P9-CDO-700

To My Irish Friend

Andy Hannigan

Glad our paths crossed!
Continued success with
your next 25 years!
in all your endeavors!

My BEST.
Patrick O'Cooley
Is. 40:31

# Flight Plan for Living

# FLIGHT PLAN FOR LIVING

## The Art of Self-Encouragement

### PATRICK O'DOOLEY

Copyright © 1992 by Patrick O'Dooley

All rights reserved, including the right
of reproduction in whole or
in part in any form.

**Library of Congress Cataloging-in-Publication Data**
O'Dooley, Patrick.
    Flight plan for living : the art of self-encouragement / Patrick O'Dooley.
        p.    cm.
    ISBN 0-942361-55-5
    1. Conduct of life.  2. Self-help techniques.  I. Title.
    II. Title: Self-encouragement.
    BF637.C5037   1992                                        92-18245
    158'.1—dc20                                                  CIP

Designed by Jacqueline Schuman
Manufactured in the United States of America
10 9 8 7 6 5 4 3 2

To my dad, Clyde, who taught me persistence.

To my mother, Dorothy, who encouraged me.

To my wife and partner, Beverly, who loved me and helped me grow.

To my son and daughter, Kelly and Alicia, God's ultimate blessings.

# Contents

# *Flight Plan for Living*

# Introduction: A Good Reminder Is Better Than a Breakthrough

More than two hundred years ago, Samuel Johnson, the Oxford-educated English writer, said, "Mankind has a far greater need to be reminded than informed."

Most people know what they need to do in life, or they know where to look for answers. However, somehow we fail to embody even those ideas that seem life-changing to us when we read them.

Your previous encounters with "breakthrough" claims probably leave you skeptical about hearing any more. Perhaps that's because what you need now are not fresh ideas about living, but rather a reminder system that will enable you to use every day what you already know.

To be done effectively, most things in life need to be done repetitively. We can brush and floss our teeth twice daily for decades, but if we stop one day and say, "There, that ought to do it," it wouldn't be long before our teeth began to decay.

Therefore, we should not be surprised that some of the principles set out in other self-help books aren't the panacea we might have expected. If we stop brushing and flossing our lives, they, too, will begin to decay.

The need for continual input is basic. We don't need soothsaying from a guru sequestered on a mountaintop, or to figure out how our alpha waves harmonize with our beta waves. All we need is help to follow consistently those things we already believe will work best for us. *Flight Plan for Living* provides an easy-to-use system of reminders to keep us on course using what we already know.

During my years as a motivational speaker, I have collected a treasure trove of popular and effective anecdotes that illustrate simple principles of everyday living. I have presented them in this book as a guide to be used through life as surely as a pilot follows a flight plan. These stories present timeless principles, simple lessons, and observations.

I've chosen the flying analogy because I am a private pilot today and, for a time, made my living as a professional pilot. My flying experiences provided a parallel with daily life, which I will explain more fully beginning in chapter one.

### SIMPLICITY 95 PERCENT OF THE TIME

Many people tell me that neither life nor flying is simple. I disagree. I know that, in a matter of five or ten minutes, I can teach anyone — even someone who has never before been in an airplane — the skills necessary to fly a plane.

It's simple: To make the plane go up, you pull back on the control wheel; to go down, you push forward. Turning left or right is no more difficult than turning a car. Within minutes, you would be proficient enough to fly across the country . . . unless you needed to stop for fuel or to land when you reached your destination.

Yes, flying across the country is easy, as long as you don't encounter bad weather, need fuel, develop an in-flight emergency, and yours is the only plane in the sky. Life is just as simple, as long as you can cruise through it in favorable conditions.

As in flying, life becomes complex when you encounter turbulent weather or emergencies, when you need fuel to land at a planned or unplanned destination, or when you share your personal sky with other people who are crowding your airspace.

When people learn to fly, 95 percent of their training focuses on how to handle situations that take up only about 5 percent of flight time. What pilots do most of the time is cruise, yet little time is devoted to this simple aspect of piloting a plane.

We need to apply the same methods to living, allocating planning time to practice for the emergencies we will face, planning our reserves and alternatives, and allowing for strong headwinds. We may not need them often, but our planning and practice will dramatically improve how easily we handle the bad weather and headwinds of life.

## WHAT ARE YOU SPEEDING TOWARD?

During the twentieth century, we have steadily increased the speed at which we live. We do more, hear more, see more, and say more — especially in America — than any civilization before us. Nevertheless, most people feel they do not have enough time, despite all the time-saving devices in our lives, and even though we have more options and opportunities than ever.

I have a friend who learned to skate when he was young. The first time he was on the ice he discovered that he had a natural ability to skate very fast. Soon he was skating faster than anybody you've ever seen; he really tore up the ice. The problem was that he didn't know how to turn or to stop gracefully. He was unable to play hockey or to figure skate, but he could cut a straight line in the ice like a buzz saw. He's much older now, and he can still impress people with his speed on the ice — until he has to coast to a stop or grab the railing to avoid flying head over heels over the top of it.

He's a good illustration why today's fast-paced life is not rewarding: There's more to life than increasing its speed.

I had a similar experience when I was introduced to snow skiing. I went with some friends to Breckenridge, Colorado, because I was told it had a long downhill run that would make it easy for me to learn.

The first time I strapped on a pair of skis I fell over backward. There I was, flat on my back in the middle of the parking lot, surrounded by people laughing at me because I was already out of control. After I learned how to pick myself up and stay on my feet, a friend took me to the top of the downhill run. My friend said, "Point your skis down the hill, Patrick, and you'll have a long, easy slope with lots of room at the end to slow down and stop."

Before I knew it, I was having the thrill of my life. The exhilaration of skiing so fast brought tears to my eyes. I loved the sensation of the long, straight run, on a hill where there were few other people. Toward the bottom, I came to the long, gradual transition my friend had promised, and I easily came to a safe and comfortable stop. Naturally, I was very proud of myself, so I jumped on the next lift and spent the rest of the day racing down the mountain as many times as I could. By the time darkness forced me to quit, I was pretty confident I could handle nearly anything on skis.

The next day, my group went to Vail for some variety. I went immediately to the top but, once there, I found that the runs were quite different. They required many turns and much more control of my skis, and there was no gentle transition at the end for easy stopping. That was one of the longest days of my life, as I literally fell down the mountain little by little. All the speed I had attained the day before did me no good when I had to turn and stop and make adjustments.

Flying through life is a lot like my first skiing experience. It's easy to learn how to coast downhill, but successful living also requires turning and stopping and sharing your mountain with other people.

The same tunnel vision often can be seen in the relationships between spouses. I continually run into couples who are enormously happy together and they go along for years with everyone they know admiring them for their model relationship. Then, without warning, all their friends are aghast to hear that their relationship is over. What's the problem? Everyone thought they were so happy together. How could they be getting a divorce?

When you think about it, you realize that almost anybody can make things work for cruising on autopilot, the 95 percent of the time when everything goes well. It's the other 5 percent of life that makes the difference between a happy marriage and one that crashes and burns.

Couples often get by for years by ignoring the daily problems they encounter, thinking they are building a strong relationship because they never have spats. This is like ignoring preventive maintenance in an airplane, because when something does go wrong, the built-in backups are gone and the relationship comes to a sudden and catastrophic end. Had the marriage been filled with continual attention to the small things as they emerged, the couple could have flown safely through the turbulence of a major disagreement later.

Anybody can handle the 95 percent of life that is routine. However, building resilience and gaining the skills to handle life's inevitable turbulence decrease our vulnerability to smashing into that mountain of troubles when it appears in front of us. After all, speeding through life doesn't seem to provide the fulfillment that many people once thought it would.

## ANTICIPATING PROBLEMS

Speed brought remarkable changes to the airlines and to the careers of many professional pilots. Before the jet engine was placed into commercial service, the grand old "Queens of the Sky" were pulled through the air by growling engines at speeds that then seemed fast. However, those DC-6s, DC-7s, and Constellations were never so fast that their pilots had difficulty keeping up with them.

That was all changed by the jet engine. Many seasoned veterans of the propeller era were unable to make the transition to jet transports, because they couldn't adjust their thinking to meet the demands of the higher speeds. Some excellent pilots were forced into early retirement as jets began to rule the nation's commercial airways.

Until jets entered service, it was not necessary to plan a flight as carefully or as far in advance. The slower airplanes allowed pilots to react to each eventuality as it came up. The jets required projecting oneself mentally into the future to prepare in the present for situations that might come up later. In a jet, if one waits until the need for action is obvious, it is nearly always too late.

One simple example of this is the descent and landing phases of the propeller aircraft compared with those of the jet plane. In a prop plane, the pilot could watch out the window for the airport to appear, then throttle back and lower the nose. The fat, straight wings of those old airplanes gave them a high degree of aerodynamic drag. That drag combined with wide propellers on the idling engines would slow a plane rapidly. Furthermore, the descent brought little discomfort to its passengers' ears because the planes were never up very high when the descent began.

In contrast, jet planes have much lower aerodynamic drag and their jet engines put out more thrust when idling than many old propeller engines did at peak power. It takes many miles to slow a modern jet airliner, and the descent is further complicated by the jet's high cruise altitude.

Jet airliners typically begin their descent about one hundred miles from the destination airport, well before it can be seen by the pilot. If the pilot waited until the airport was clearly in view before slowing or descending, he would be what we call "high and fast," a double whammy in a jet airplane. Being "high and fast" in a jet would require a great deal of circling and an uncomfortably high rate of descent that is hard on the ears of the passengers.

Life today has passed from the graceful days of propeller airplanes to the blazing speed of jets. Notice I said "life," because it's not limited to flying. In a sense, nearly everything we do today is jet-propelled and there will be no going back to the slower ways. Many people are like the old veteran propeller pilots, though, not having made the transition to a new way of thinking. While those older pilots were allowed to take early retirement, it's much more difficult to retire from life.

## GETTING YOUR FLIGHT PLAN READY

So, how do you adjust comfortably and easily to the jet speeds of your everyday life? That's how this book can help. It will show you how to use many of the techniques used by pilots of today's high-speed jets. It will help you to plan ahead and take actions in anticipation of what may be a pressing need later. We'll explore how to navigate well enough through life that you won't fly past your destinations in life because you were caught "high and fast." Nor will you be forced into making a sudden and uncomfortable descent, or, worst of all, crashing catastrophically.

As you proceed through each chapter, if you feel you have read something like this before, I invite you to recall the opening quotation from Samuel Johnson: "Mankind has a far greater need to be reminded than informed." I will be your co-pilot on your flight toward a new and better destination in your life. As the captain on this trip, it's up to you to make the applications to your own life.

*The aviation term* clear on top *means you have climbed above all the clouds and are flying in clear skies with the stormy weather below you.*

# 1
# FLYING "CLEAR ON TOP"

I can't think of any institution in today's society that is as successful as commercial flying. I'm not talking about the current temporary financial problems that have brought on mergers and takeovers. I'm not talking about the delays that are experienced due to traffic congestion and weather problems. I'm talking about the actual flight operation of taking off and landing a modern jet airliner.

If you look at the statistics, you will see that commercial aviation is one of the most phenomenally successful endeavors ever undertaken by humankind. Your chance of dying in a plane crash is about 1 in 2,600,000. What else in our society offers such safety odds in your favor?

What's behind this enviable safety record is the contribution of the pilots and ground crew, who are rigorously trained to go through checklists at all stages of flight. They would consider a success rate of 99.9 percent to be disastrous. Their goal is to have 100 percent of all flights arrive safely. Losses are simply not tolerated.

You can apply to your daily life the same care and preparation that commercial pilots and ground crews use before, during, and after a flight. The key is to prepare in advance to ensure that your checklists are comprehensive enough to anticipate emergencies. Then go over your plans with people who care about the success of your personal flight through life, and modify your procedures to achieve the maximum potential for success.

As if to illustrate the safety of today's aircraft and flying procedures, witness the air war in the Persian Gulf. There, in the hostile environment of a combat theater, American forces operated more than 110,000 flights while losing only a handful of aircraft. The environment there was extraordinarily dangerous, yet the losses were low.

One thing you can bet your life on — and thousands of our U.S. military personnel did — is that every one of those flights was carefully planned and operated according to strict rules and controls. Especially in combat, safety is enhanced dramatically by following checklists.

A major benefit of using checklists is that they are prepared when things are calm and you have time to think things through. The action items on a flight plan are written with the expertise and guidance of experienced engineers and pilots when there are no time constraints. Then, in the heat of a crisis, when mistakes are likely to be made, the pilot can simply perform by rote a checklist of actions in their proper order.

The flying metaphor will serve you well as a guide to life if you plan your personal checks and go through them as diligently as a professional jet pilot.


## BECOMING A SELF-ENCOURAGER

People today seem ready, willing, and able to dispense advice to others and often they are able to see things that their friends or families may miss. However, it's interesting that as good as we may be at helping others, most of us are not good at giving ourselves advice.

We frequently view our own problems as insurmountable because we lack the objectivity we have when we are thinking about someone else's problems. We also fail to give ourselves the same measure of self-encouragement as we offer to others. Instead, we tend to beat up on ourselves and say things to ourselves that we would never say to someone else. In other words, we rarely treat ourselves as well as we treat our friends, or even as well as we treat complete strangers.

When you become your own most encouraging voice, you never have to count on an external source to do it. If you get regular, ego-building encouragement from others, that's great, but even your most dedicated fans will not be there all the time, or be able to help you out with all the discouraging things that you think about but never express openly.

The ability to be your own champion is something I call *self-encouragement*. The self-encourager understands the beauty of flying *clear on top* by pushing through to climb above the turbulence in life. It's a term you won't yet find in the dictionary, but once you become a self-encourager, you will find your life flying along much more smoothly than ever before.

## *INTO THE CLEARING*

Every pilot, no matter how seasoned, likes the feeling of breaking out on top of a layer of clouds into clear blue skies. Even veteran airline pilots — for whom instrument flying comes as easily as driving a car — enjoy flying by visual references with unlimited visibility. It's always more comfortable to see outside and forget the instruments for a while.

Though we always prefer clear sailing, inevitably life requires us to fly in the clouds some of the time. When an airplane flies through clouds, visibility is restricted and the weather usually causes a bumpy ride. As pilots climb through the clouds, they know that somewhere above it's clear on top and that the bouncing and jarring will not last forever. Eventually, the reward for climbing will be breaking out on top into smoother air.

Imagine now that you are a jet pilot, able to fly high and fast. Put yourself mentally into the cockpit and come with me on a jet-powered flight through your life.

To a pilot who is experiencing a jarring climb through rain clouds, one of the most welcome sights in the world is the ethereal beauty of perfect blue skies above and the soft cotton of the cloudtops below. Perched high above the clouds, the pilot knows that, underneath the white beauty, people may be getting drenched under a dark, gray mess of gloomy skies. You could be down there in the storm, wishing you were above the weather. If wishing is all you ever do, that's where you will remain.

Instead, you take off and climb right into the heart of the storm, taking a pounding worse than if you had remained on the ground. Finally, you are rewarded for your courage in struggling through the mass of grayness. When the bumping and jarring and being tossed around is over, you can relax and enjoy the fruits of your efforts.

Climbing through the storms in our lives, we must continue to pursue the blue skies above. At times, your personal flight conditions may be worse than if you had stayed safely on the ground huddled in a hangar, but by venturing out you've given yourself the opportunity to see sunshine on an otherwise rainy day.

As a self-encourager, you can expect to experience more good days and fewer bad days than most people because you will be able to climb above life's clouds. However, even when you're flying clear on top, conditions other than clouds will continue to affect your life. You will find that your daily speed is different, some days doing better than others, even though you may be in the clear. When your speed varies from day to day, you are experiencing the effect of headwinds and tailwinds.

## FACTOR IN THE WINDS OF LIFE

All airplanes have an optimum cruising speed at which the plane achieves its highest efficiency level. However, the plane's speed through the air is rarely the same as its speed across the ground. Even when flying in the clear, the ground speed of an airplane is changed dramatically by the winds aloft.

Flying into a headwind results in a lower ground speed, while flying with a tailwind results in a ground speed higher than the plane is able to fly without wind. Think of your ground speed in

*11*

life as the sum of your speed and the speed of your surrounding environment. A tailwind increases your apparent speed and a headwind decreases it.

When flying an aircraft, we cannot choose a headwind or a tailwind. If the winds are from the west and you're flying west today, you take on extra fuel, plan a refueling stop, allow for the extra time, and go anyway. We can operate our lives the same way by planning for personal headwinds. The important thing to understand is the principle, and to check which way the wind is blowing before you depart.

### Checking the Headwinds

One example of a good time to watch the winds would be when you start a business. If the economy is souring or your industry is suffering a financial downturn, you are flying into a headwind. Before launching your business, calculate whether you have enough capital to fuel your business until the headwind subsides.

You may decide that you can make it safely despite the headwind. There can be advantages in doing that: if you succeed, even though you will have fought harder and used more fuel, you will arrive ahead of your competitors, many of whom will not fly to where you are until the winds turn more favorable. By then, you may have your business soundly established.

Perhaps you are considering taking a night course to further your education. If you simply made a spur-of-the-moment decision to enroll, you might have been surprised when your business demands suddenly increased and you were flying into the night course with a headwind too strong to overcome. You realize too late that you cannot reach your destination with the fuel you have on board. You may have to turn back or make a refueling stop.

Refueling stops are inefficient because they always burn more fuel than flying nonstop. Stopping requires fuel for an approach pattern, landing, and taxi-in, an extra engine start and taxi-out for takeoff, plus the fuel needed to climb back up to altitude. If you know which way the wind is blowing, you can decide whether you can afford the extra fuel or whether, by waiting until the winds improve, you can go nonstop.

*Watching for Tailwinds*

Being aware of the winds will enable you to spot a favorable tailwind and take off when others think, "That's too far, you'll crash short of your destination." An example of this is Kevin Costner's movie project *Dances with Wolves*.

Many of his associates in the industry thought he was taking off for a crash landing that would ruin his career. They might have been right had the movie been released a couple of years earlier, because the winds did not favor the destination that Costner chose.

However, Costner demonstrated the winds aloft principle; he knew there was a tailwind at the altitude of "a western movie." He took off on a flight (his movie) that was much longer than anyone thought could succeed, and he reached his destination because of a tailwind that no one else knew existed. Now, because Costner has already arrived, others are frantically fueling up and taking off for the same destination. Some of them may make it, but none will likely succeed as well as Costner.

Everyone remembers the first of a genre like *Dances with Wolves*, but few will recall those that come next. Who was the second person to fly solo across the Atlantic Ocean? Who was the first person to set foot on the moon on the *second* lunar landing mission?

*Ignoring the Forecast*

Consider the case of another movie released about the same time as *Dances with Wolves*. Instead of finding favorable winds, *The Flight of the Intruder* launched into the headwind of a real war in the Persian Gulf. Suddenly, no one was interested in seeing a movie about a subject that engulfed them every time they turned on the TV or opened a newspaper.

There was substantial advance warning about the headwind encountered by *The Flight of the Intruder*. There were the reports of the United Nations' resolutions, which were followed by the long buildup of allied forces. The movie's producer had the equivalent of winds aloft weather reports, but failed to adjust the timing of the picture's release accordingly.

Fortunately, we are not strictly at the mercy of the prevailing winds when heading for a destination. It is possible to take action that will have a great impact on the result of the winds we encounter. For example, the winds vary considerably with altitude, which is a critical factor in flight planning for high-flying jets.

All jets have an optimum cruising altitude at which they get the greatest distance out of every gallon of fuel. However, the optimum altitude for a particular plane is calculated without factoring in wind effects. A pilot may discover that the optimum altitude has a 100-knot headwind and that a lower, slightly less efficient altitude has only a 50-knot headwind. Therefore, although the type of aircraft may have an optimum altitude, the plane's efficiency *on that particular flight* will be better at the lower altitude. Resourceful pilots do lots of "what-if" calculations to consider taking altitudes that would normally not make sense.

You will often see the same techniques used in business through the "what-if" revelations of computer spreadsheets. When running those hypothetical scenarios on your computer, do you add or subtract factors for life's headwinds and tailwinds? Do your competitors? Why not search now for destinations that your plane might reach if only you had the proper tailwind? Get the flight plan ready now with the tailwind already figured in, and when the tailwind you need is forecast, fuel up and go. You may be, as Kevin Costner was, the only one flying that day.

*FLY AT YOUR OWN OPTIMUM LEVEL*

The principles that pilots apply to choosing their cruising altitude also apply to our daily lives. As we fly through life, there are different levels for different people, even for the same people at different times. There is no dishonor in taking the proper altitude, yet our society is stuck on the idea that higher is always better.

Sometimes people find that the rarefied air of the stratosphere is not what they expected. Consider the junk bond kings of only a few years ago. They thought they would have a wonderful, high-flying life. Instead, it's been cold, the headwinds are stronger than they imagined, and most will be lucky to survive.

Many planes that were designed to fly comfortably at lower altitudes offer certain advantages. Though you will not reach your destination as quickly, the process of getting there can itself be an enjoyable part of the trip. At lower altitudes you can open a window, or at least look out and enjoy the land below.

Unfortunately, many people in today's fast-paced society feel that time en route is time wasted. It's as if their lives don't exist while they travel. There *is* more to life than increasing its speed. Are you flying at your personal optimum altitude, or are you trying to emulate the high-fliers you see around you?

Even professional jet pilots can get caught up in ego-centered attempts to stretch their capabilities. Many years ago, the Cessna Aircraft Corporation, best known for its line of small aircraft, jumped into the higher-flying world of corporate jets when it produced a twin-engine model called the Citation. Cessna Citations are a cross between typical Cessna aircraft and the blinding performance of the famed LearJet, resulting in a jet-powered aircraft without the speed and altitude capabilities of any other business jet on the market.

Some Citation pilots were embarrassed to have other jet pilots hear them over the radio calling air traffic control to check in at lower altitudes. They knew no one would be favorably impressed by a relatively low-flying Citation. To alleviate their embarrassment, some would push the performance margins of the Citation to the limits and operate the airplane inefficiently simply to be able to call in a higher — and presumably more impressive — altitude. The danger in operating close to the plane's performance margins is that a little turbulence could upset the plane and put it into a stall situation that could cause it to tumble out of the sky.

The only pilots who might have been impressed by the high-flying Citation pilots were those in lower-flying planes; unfortunately, lower-flying planes are on other frequencies and cannot hear the Citation pilots anyway. Those on the same frequency as the Citations were in higher-performance planes and were probably thinking that they'd hate to be up in a Citation, hanging on to the edge of its performance margins.

Conversely, I believe that those who leverage what they've got are respected by everyone. Trying to climb higher than you are truly capable can be a prescription for disaster. No matter how high you go, there will always be someone else flying higher. If you build your ego on trying to fly higher than everyone else, you may exceed your performance margins and come tumbling out of the sky.

Here's a quotation I saw on a bulletin board in the Dallas Cowboys' locker room: *The quality of a person's life is in direct proportion to their commitment to excellence — no matter what their field of endeavor.*

That was said by the great football coach Vince Lombardi, who took a group of losers and, by encouraging them to believe in themselves and their skills, helped them become world champions. Winning requires both great skill and a tremendous attitude.

Doing the best at whatever it is you do is more important than the field of endeavor. Look at all the people who follow the Special Olympics. They applaud wildly for athletes whose performances would be embarrassing in other arenas. The cheers at a Special Olympics event are for people who are doing the most with what they have — that's what earns respect.

We are all blessed with different skills. You can always operate at your optimum level if you have the judgment to assess what you've got and make the most of it by constantly fine-tuning your cruising altitude.

## BE WILLING TO CHANGE ALTITUDE

When you become a successful self-encourager, you will notice how many people tend to stay at their current altitude. They may

*16*

not even look for better winds down low. Instead, they stay in their well-worn and familiar rut, even if that rut is not particularly comfortable or safe.

Good pilots always update winds-aloft reports while en route to see if new ones have come in. They may have based their flight plan on winds-aloft reports forecast early in the day. Later, if other aircraft find the forecast to be wrong, their pilots are encouraged to report these differences via radio to Flight Service Stations on the ground. Thus, by radioing to Flight Service Stations to report changes and receive updates, a pilot may adjust altitude en route for better efficiency.

This may result in the discovery of unexpectedly favorable winds, or it may warn of higher-than-forecast headwinds. If the actual winds are so much worse that the plane no longer has enough fuel, and if the pilot failed to keep updated until it was too late, the flight might be jeopardized by the pilot's inability to recover gracefully.

How might you change altitude in life? More than 90 percent of the people in America live on 3 percent of its land mass. Some people will remain stuck in the rat race of a big city while opportunities go begging in other parts of the country. So, if you move, you might be doing in your life the equivalent of a pilot changing altitude to find a stronger tailwind.

We can all have the equivalent of winds-aloft reports. Financial newsletters, magazines, even the daily newspaper can tell us of changing winds. Just because you took off in favorable conditions doesn't mean you should avoid being vigilant about changes. You may learn that staying where you are will leave you short of fuel, but that changing altitude temporarily will enable you to continue.

## ATTITUDE IS THE KEY TO SUCCESS

The most basic of all flight instruments — the one that is most critical for keeping a plane flying properly in all kinds of weather — is the attitude indicator, also known as the artificial horizon indicator. The attitude indicator, like your personal attitude, is the most important instrument in maintaining control. In a plane, the attitude indicator shows whether you are going up or down or whether you are turning. Your personal attitude defines how you look at life, which in turn determines how well you fly through it.

In life as in flying, when things are going well, we don't need an attitude indicator. On a clear day, when weather conditions are reported as ceiling and visibility unlimited (CAVU), you can fly visually with no need for an attitude indicator. The planet earth is your horizon and, from your lofty perch, you can easily distinguish right side up. When flying in the clouds, however, your life depends on maintaining the proper attitude and you've got to depend on and live by your attitude indicator. The same applies to life; the worse the weather, the more you need to focus on the attitude indicator.

A good attitude tends to perpetuate itself and, unfortunately, so does a bad one. It's the same in flying: When you are straight and level and you see the plane roll a degree or two, you can easily correct and put it straight. If you take your eyes off your attitude indicator for too long, though, you may find that you have deviated too far to correct. It's the continual small corrections that are crucial.

When flying an airplane in the clouds, you cannot sense when it rolls over. You can lose track of your attitude to such a degree that you cannot recover. You may become so confused that you attempt a correction that is the opposite of what is needed. A leading researcher, Roger Bárány, developed a demonstration to show pilots how disoriented they could become when deprived of visual references.

The U.S. Air Force uses the Bárány Chair during pilot training. The chair is like a short bar stool that spins freely on its stand. Pilots in training are strapped into the chair and blindfolded. Then they are instructed to hold their arms in front of them and use their thumbs to indicate the direction of rotation.

At first everyone's thumbs point straight up. As the chair is spun, the trainees' thumbs point in the correct direction until equilibrium is established with the fluids in their inner ears. Then the chair is slowed slightly, and because the trainees "sense" that they have stopped, their thumbs will be held straight up. The chair is slowed a second time and because the fluids in the inner ear are giving false signals, the trainees will point their thumbs in the opposite direction from their true direction of rotation.

When the blindfold is removed with the chair spinning in a direction opposite the position of their thumbs, the trainees experience one of the most disorienting and confusing moments of their lives. People are not normally confused in a spinning chair, because their eyes provide sensory feedback to correct the erroneous signals from the inner ear.

Once having seen this demonstration, pilots will never forget to scan their instruments diligently. Even if their inner senses send signals that contradict the information on the attitude indicator, good instrument pilots will continue to hold a proper attitude.

We need to observe the same principle in life that instrument pilots do in a plane. No matter how confusing and disorienting things seem to get, we've got to rely on our attitudes to fly through the tough times. Maintaining a positive attitude helps to keep us focused on the big picture. Failure to follow the attitude indicator's information has been the cause of countless fatal aircraft accidents.

Most aviation accidents occur during takeoff and landing. Among those that occur during a cruising flight, the worst occur when inexperienced pilots let their attitude get too far off. Then, when they try to correct their attitude, they find themselves in a steep dive, and their instinct to yank hard on the controls may further jeopardize the aircraft.

Even a small adjustment to the controls when you're pushing your speed limit can make large changes in attitude and put major stress on the plane. Therefore, an abrupt yank on the controls exerts more pressure than you might imagine and more than the plane may be able to handle.

When things get way out of whack for us, we often try to overcorrect by yanking things apart that we might have salvaged with more gentle corrections. Of course, the best technique is a regular scan of your attitude so it never gets too far out of line. If it does go a little farther than you'd like, then remember to correct gently back to a positive attitude because your life may be operating in a highly sensitive mode.

In every aspect of your life — relationships with your children, your spouse, business associates, or with your finances — keep a good attitude and avoid getting lazy while things are going well. When life is cruising along in the clear, you may be able to let things roll back and forth a bit without paying a lot of attention. Even if you rolled far astray of straight and level, if the ride in your life is smooth, you probably can correct easily.

The problem arises when you have not been maintaining a good attitude and you hit some turbulence. Suddenly, the few degrees you were off is amplified and you are now faced with the need to correct your attitude in turbulent air. That's a combination with a deadly potential.

The weather will usually get better if you are persistent and fly through the rough air. Remember, somewhere it's always *clear on top.* Inevitably we will have to go through difficult times in our lives, and usually they will get better. Attitude is the most important instrument in the airplane, just as it is in life.

You will see your attitude improving as you gain skill at being a self-encourager. Don't be discouraged; your progress toward self-encouragement will get better with time and practice.

## DON'T GIVE UP

In the early days of flying, attitude indicators worked crudely. They indicated the correct aircraft attitude for brief periods of time, and then they had to be reset by the pilot. This resetting was called *caging* the attitude indicator.

To cage the attitude indicator while in flight, the pilot had to level the wings and fly straight ahead for a few seconds, then pull the caging knob to reorient the attitude indicator to the proper horizon. These old attitude indicators were especially vulnerable to aggressive maneuvering, causing them to tumble and become completely useless. Of course, such wild maneuvers were normally restricted to clear flight conditions, so that the pilot was able to level the plane out when finished with the maneuver and recage the attitude indicator.

As technology improved, gyroscope companies were able to produce attitude indicators that reset themselves automatically. Today, pilots never need to recage their attitude indicators, regardless of the length of the flight. Today's high-tech attitude indicators are unaffected by turbulence or aggressive maneuvering. Instead of tumbling out of control or drifting off kilter, today's aircraft gyroscopes make constant small corrections to keep oriented to the true horizon.

Your first efforts at self-encouragement and maintaining a positive attitude may be similar to the workings of early aircraft attitude indicators, needing to be recaged from time to time. If so, slow your maneuvering and level out for a bit so you can reorient yourself.

Especially in the beginning stages of self-encouragement, only attempt something highly unusual when the weather is good. For example, you might be cautious at first with your finances so that your life has relatively smooth sailing. If your attitude indicator tumbles when you are flying through clear financial skies, you will be able to see where the horizon is and manually lower your landing gear.

Once you become proficient at self-encouragement and have developed a late-model attitude indicator, you will find that you can reset yourself automatically. You will make constant small corrections in your attitude throughout every aspect of your life. When you have become self-adjusting, you will be powerful enough to fly through nearly any weather that comes your way, and you will be ready to fly to nearly any destination you choose.

*Every flight has a destination, even if it's the same airport from which the plane took off. Most flights have the clear objective of flying from Point A to Point B. For either local or cross-country flying, the pilot has a mission in mind and a place to land when the plane needs refueling.*

## 2
# CHOOSING YOUR DESTINATION

One of the great thrills in flying is to take off for a destination that you've never been to before. It's a strange sensation the first time out. After reading all the data about the new airport, you use aviation charts to plan your route and to plot checkpoints along the way. By following your flight path, by using the proper checklists and crossing your planned checkpoints, the new airport will soon appear before you. Here's how the same procedures can be applied to your life.

Your destination in life is your vision of where you most want to be at some future time. Knowing your target and filing a flight plan will help you keep focused on your goals. You might file the flight plan of your life's destination with a friend, a spouse, or with your parents. There is tremendous power in making a public declaration of your goal. In the next chapter, we will talk more about filing a flight plan, but first we need to concentrate on a destination.

## *CAUTION: BEWARE OF* GET-THERE-ITIS

Once they have chosen a destination for their lives, many people become riveted on reaching their destination at all costs. Although there are tons of books out today telling people "you can do anything" so "go for it," there are limits. I am sure that I'm not going to be an NBA basketball star or play in the Super Bowl. These are the facts of my own limitations. "Can do" books often fail to address practical and obvious human boundaries.

Sometimes, the best judgment is to cancel the flight or change the destination. A professional pilot will do these things without question to ensure the safety of the flight. If you go through life with the idea of "getting there at all costs," then be prepared for life to demand that ultimate payment.

There is an aviation cliché that the most dangerous thing in the air is the doctor in a Bonanza. Beechcraft Bonanzas, the Mercedes-Benzes of the air, are frequently owned by successful and busy professionals such as doctors. The combination of an impatient person and a highly capable airplane has led to disaster when pilots have pushed beyond what they could handle when they applied their "can do" attitude to flying.

The disease that afflicts pilots who operate like a doctor in a Bonanza is called *Get-There-itis.* Pilots with Get-There-itis gamble by betting the ultimate stake that they will make it to their destination.

Blind dedication to reaching a destination may bear a high cost for you and for the careers, livelihoods, relationships, or financial security of others whose well-being has been entrusted to you.

In the movie *Out of Africa,* there is a great scene where the heroine, played by Meryl Streep, takes a risky trip into the wilderness and has a close encounter with a lion. Later, in questioning aloud her reason for placing herself in such jeopardy, the movie's hero, played by Robert Redford, offers sage advice. "It's all right to take a chance," he says, "as long as you're the only one who will pay."

Few people embark on a venture knowing that they are risking their lives. Pilots always believe they are skilled enough to handle all flight conditions, even when they have not accurately assessed them. Sometimes they realize that the conditions will press their limits for a while, but they expect improvement down the road that will allow clear flying. So they initiate the flight thinking that they will only be on the edge for a short time. However, this expectation fails to address the possibility that conditions may be worse than expected, or won't improve, or may worsen as the flight progresses.

Get-There-itis usually results from the perception that there's an incredibly important reason for taking a big risk. Doctors in Bonanzas have no monopoly on Get-There-itis; it can happen even to professional airline pilots.

A pilot for a major airline was on the return trip with his family in a small aircraft. The weather was terrible all along the route of flight as well as at his destination. At a refueling stop, where he was fortunate to land safely, he was advised against going on. He said, "I have to get back today because I have a scheduled airline flight tomorrow morning. I'm new and still on probation, so if I don't get there on time they'll fire me for missing the trip."

He completed his refueling and took off on the last leg home, but the warning he'd received proved to be true. The pilot and his whole family perished in the crash.

Sadly, we've now got a whole country full of people afflicted with Get-There-itis. The disease takes many forms but the results are basically the same: everybody wants everything instantly. We've become a remote-control TV society and we sometimes forget that there are limitations — some things truly are not possible, or at least not instantly attainable.

Failing to recognize one's limitations is bound to result in trouble. Sometimes it takes courage to face reality and to delay your trip, choose an alternate destination, or wait out unfavorable conditions.

## *YOU'VE GOT TO LOG THE HOURS*

Suppose you knew someone who quit his job to start his own business. Suppose you used that example as inspiration to tell your boss to "take this job and shove it." Then, by the time your new business was failing, you learned that your role model had spent years building his reputation, client base, and savings account before quitting his job.

The reason people take on more than they can handle is frequently that they fail to realize all the effort necessary to attain a goal. To reach the desired destination, you must develop the skills or acquire the tools to do it.

Today's jet airliners can fly in nearly any weather because they carry top-of-the-line equipment operated by well-trained and experienced pilots. Private pilots, on the other hand, have less training and experience, and usually fly aircraft that are less fully equipped than jetliners.

If we select our destination in life based on where top-of-the-line professionals are, but we take off toward that destination in a small, poorly equipped aircraft after little training and no recent practice, we may not make it to our goal.

The NBA basketball star "Pistol Pete" Maravich was the most talented ball-handler in professional basketball. Many young basketball players have tried to emulate him, but have been frustrated by their inability to perform as Maravich did.

Maravich was not born with those skills. He worked very hard to build them. He was so dedicated to his practice that he even would dribble a basketball from an aisle seat in a movie theater, so he could develop unprecedented ball-handling capabilities.

Anyone who attempted to match Maravich's talents without going through the rigorous discipline he applied would be frustrated. It isn't enough merely to watch Maravich play and think, "If he can do that, I can do that." You have to pay the price to make a dream come true, dribbling a ball during countless movies to develop the skills of a Maravich.

## NOWHERE TO GO

It used to be much easier to choose a destination, because social mores nearly always demanded conformity. Many people were led to their destinations by the expectations of others. Often, it wasn't one's dream destination, but at least it was a destination.

Today, however, it is more acceptable to be a drifter. There are so many options to choose from that some people simply cannot focus on one destination and stick with it.

When I was in college, something happened to me that demonstrates the changes in social mores over the last two decades. I established a tradition of sorts with two of my best friends. Each summer, we threw a big party for our friends at a lake near Dallas. We rented a barge and hired a band and made it a really big event to which everyone looked forward.

The summer after my sophomore year, when I was working at the Rock Island Railroad, there was a special girl in my life named Beverly May. We had met at college before summer vacation and I was dying to see her again, but she lived in Oklahoma City and I was working in Illinois. I missed her so terribly that, halfway through the summer, I knew I had to find a way to see her.

Although I didn't have money for a flight to Dallas, I knew that the annual lake gathering would be a great time to see Beverly May. Because I worked for the Rock Island Railroad, I was able to get to Oklahoma City, a trip of twenty-one hours from Rock Island, Illinois, in a steamy caboose. Beverly May picked me up at the freight yard and then we drove together down to Dallas for the lake party.

We had a wonderful time at the lake party, and I was in heaven getting to spend the time with Beverly May. After the party, she drove me back to the Oklahoma City freight yard. However, the youthful energy and incomparable draw of a new girlfriend that had sustained me during the twenty-one-hour ride to see Beverly May completely deserted me during the twenty-one sweltering hours of the return trip.

The train left at eight o'clock at night. I was exhausted from the day and hoped that sleeping would help pass the hours. The guys in the caboose made a place for me to lie down on a hard, oak bench, which faithfully reproduced every rattle of the caboose. That would have been bad enough, but the tail end of a freight train passes through all the dust and dirt that the rest of the train kicks up as it rumbles through dry, sun-baked countryside. This was not an environment even remotely conducive to sleeping.

After what seemed like forever on that bench, I felt the train stop. It was about three o'clock in the morning, but I got up because somebody came around and said, "Okay, this is it. The end of the line." I thought that I had gotten lucky and that the train had gone straight back to Rock Island. I asked, "Are we in Rock Island already?"

The guy looked at me strangely and said, "No, this is Haynes, Kansas."

"What about Rock Island?" I asked.

"The train gets broken up here," he told me, "then they'll put some new trains together and you can eventually find one going to Rock Island."

There I was, in the middle of Kansas at three in the morning with only a couple of dollars to my name and no idea of how or when I would get a ride back to Rock Island. I had no place to sleep, so I decided to walk into town to see if I could find a bite to eat or get some coffee and find a quiet, clean place to sit down.

I didn't get far on my walk before a police car pulled over and the officer asked me what I was doing. I told him I had just gotten off the train and I was looking for a place to get a cup of coffee. He knew there were no passenger trains coming through his town, especially at this time of night, so he figured I was a vagrant and up to no good. The rather light status of my personal funds helped a great deal to cement this image in his mind. He decided that the best place for me was in his local jail, and there I went.

Luckily, before he locked me up, he asked me if I knew anybody in Kansas. I remembered that I had a college buddy who lived in Wichita. The policeman let me call Terry Schreiner at five in the morning so he could verify that he knew me and that I was a college student. He also corroborated my story about where I was working for the summer, so the police officer took me back to the freight yard.

The next morning, I found a passenger train going my way, so I got on it and sat down. When the conductor came around to ask for my ticket, I showed him my Rock Island Railroad identification. He told me that my employment with Rock Island did not entitle me to ride on a passenger train, and that I would have to buy a ticket.

I explained what I had been through and how much money I had, and the conductor let me stay on. The guy sitting next to me had heard the whole story and, when he realized I wouldn't even be able to eat until we got to Rock Island, he shared his lunch with me.

Things have changed a lot since that summer adventure of mine. I was nearly locked up for the "crime" of walking around in the middle of the night with no place to stay and no money in my pocket. Today, you can go across the street from the White House in our nation's capital and find hundreds of people who live like that. The streets of New York are estimated to have more than seventy thousand street people wandering around with no place to stay for the night. Not only are they not hauled in for vagrancy, but few people even notice they're there.

So many people drift aimlessly — and even homelessly — that few will notice if you join that lost crowd. In a society that looks the other way in the face of homeless street people, being a self-encourager is crucial.

### EVERYTHING HAS ALREADY BEEN DONE

Some people don't choose a destination for their lives because they believe there is no place worthwhile left to go. I saw this phenomenon very clearly on a trip I took to North Carolina.

I've been interested in flying all my life, and I've always wanted to see Kitty Hawk, North Carolina, where the Wright Brothers took the first successful powered flight. I had been to North Carolina many times, but Kitty Hawk was way out on the coast, not easily accessible to the parts of North Carolina I usually visited. Nevertheless, every time I went there, I thought of Kitty Hawk, because I wanted to stand in the exact spot where history had occurred.

One day I got a chance to speak in Greenville, North Carolina, at a company called Grady White Boats. This company was a model of the "can do" philosophy. It had been bought by twenty-seven-year-old Grady White while it was in bankruptcy, and he built it up to be one of the largest boat companies in America. Grady resurrected the company by infusing his workers with his unbridled enthusiasm and his encouragement to build the best boats they could.

I had arranged for one of my best friends, Bill McMurrey, to pick me up after I finished speaking at Grady White Boats. Bill was also a pilot and, though he lived nearby in Charlotte, he had never been to Kitty Hawk either and wanted to see it with me.

It was wintertime and it was pouring down rain when we arrived. We stayed at a hotel nearby and we were the only ones seemingly on Kitty Hawk Island. The next day we got up, went to the exact spot where the world's first powered flight actually took place, and saw the monument to the Wright Brothers that was erected at the spot where they first flew.

I was awestruck that, here on this hill a long time ago, two bicycle mechanics were the first to achieve powered flight. They had been spat upon, cursed and called fools, and they had overcome many other obstacles to achieve that first flight of 120 feet lasting only twelve seconds. Today we can fly anywhere in the world in ultimate luxury, in planes whose wingspan is greater than the distance of that first flight.

*If God Had Wanted Man to Fly . . .*

Since the miserable winter weather did not invite a leisurely stroll, we went inside to look through the Kitty Hawk museum. There I found a startling revelation.

The museum featured an exhibit about a bishop in the United Brethren Church who became famous by going around the country telling people that the end of the world was near. He believed that the Second Coming of Christ was imminent because everything God wanted mankind to do was now done.

In 1890, someone listening to one of his sermons jumped to his feet and said, "We haven't invented everything. Someday man will learn how to fly!" The bishop's famous answer to that was "If God had wanted man to fly, He would have given him wings."

I had heard that saying for as long as I could remember, but I never knew it was a direct quotation and that someone knew the name of the man who said it. In 1903, thirteen years after he made that statement, Bishop Wright's two sons, Orville and Wilbur, delivered to the world the proof that their father was wrong. While Bishop Wright's statement suggests that we'd best not believe everything we hear, it also demonstrates that there are plenty of new and wonderful destinations awaiting your future.

There was a time when we knew so little that we didn't even know how much we didn't know. Yet, today, as advanced as our technology has become, it continually shows us that the more we know, the more we learn how much we don't know.

*How Far Is Ten Miles?*

I got a visual picture of how far we've come and how rapidly we've arrived when I was speaking in Guernsey, Wyoming. After my speech, some of the members of the audience took me outside of town to the nearby Cumberland River. This was the place where Forty-niners by the thousands came on their way to find gold in California.

They showed me ruts in the rocks where so many steel-rimmed wagons had passed that they had carved deep troughs in solid rock. When later wagons used these trails, they had to travel in ruts that were as deep as their axle hubs.

I was told that those wagon trains would only cover about ten miles on a good day. That made me think about watching the space shuttle Challenger take off; in one minute, the space shuttle climbed the entire distance it took a wagon train to travel in one good day.

Then I remembered that the top model LearJet corporate planes can cruise nearly ten miles high—again, the distance a wagon train could travel if it made good time. Indeed, the U.S. Air Force's SR-71 Blackbird reconnaissance planes, which moved faster than a bullet fired from a high-powered rifle, are no longer fast enough and have been sent into mothballed retirement.

In one lifetime, we went from Bishop Wright's statement that man would never fly to the luxury and comfort of supersonic airliners. Our destinations have changed as our technology has advanced, and I would never tell my children that everything has already been done. After all, I wouldn't want to be quoted like Bishop Wright was in the museum display honoring his sons' achievements.

## THE POWER OF VISION

My friend Ron Wagner, during his first year of pilot training in the Air Force, saw his destination as becoming an airline pilot. To reach his goal, he decided to get experience in jet transports that would be attractive to the airlines when his tour of duty was completed.

The Air Force had two airplanes that were actually civilian transports in military paint, the C-9 Nightingale hospital plane and the CT-39 Sabreliner, a twin-engine jet executive transport. Even before he arrived at his training base, Ron told friends he would get an assignment to one of those two planes when he graduated. This was a pretty bold statement because flying those planes was a highly coveted assignment and they only went to graduates who finished at the top of their flight training class. Yet, those were the planes Ron wanted to fly, and they were his destination.

### Bucking the Odds

Normally, an Air Force pilot training class is made up entirely of newly commissioned lieutenants. However, Ron began pilot training right after the war in Vietnam, so there were several

31

captains in his class who were combat veterans with extensive flight experience. Figuring that the flight experience of the combat veterans ensured them the top graduating spots, Ron quickly resigned himself to finishing no higher than fourth in his class.

The first month of Air Force pilot training is all in classrooms and involves no flying. During that first month, Ron had an experience that changed his attitude and got him once again to set his destination for the top spot in his class.

It happened when an F-106 fighter interceptor landed at Ron's training base. When a hot plane like that is around an Air Force pilot training base, news of it spreads quickly. Ron's entire class was soon on the flight line ogling this dream machine. Ron and several of his classmates were talking to a student who was graduating that week and had been assigned to fly an F-106. Ron's classmates were moaning about their misfortune to have three experienced captains in their class, and complaining that there was no way they could finish high enough to get the assignment of their dreams.

When he heard their complaints, the senior student laid into them. "Here you are, you haven't even started flying yet, and you've already given up. You have no idea how those captains will do and you've resigned yourself to finishing below them." Ron never forgot that scolding and used its energy to refocus on his destination.

*Sticking to a Flight Plan*

Once his vision was firmly reestablished, Ron was able to set up checkpoints along the way to his destination. Step by step, as his year in pilot training passed, he followed his plan. With a clear goal and a plan for reaching it, Ron systematically flew past all three captains to finish number one in his class. His efforts earned him an assignment flying the CT-39A Sabreliner executive jet transport in the Presidential Wing at Andrews Air Force Base in Washington, D.C., an assignment considered by many to be the plushest of all Air Force flight assignments.

Ron also did the equivalent of filing a flight plan for his destination by telling the other students about his goal. He told me that if he had kept his dream a secret, he might never have attained it. Instead, by declaring his mission openly, small things began to happen along the way that pushed him toward his goal. When you let others know of your intentions, you will be amazed at the help that will become available to you.

*If an aircraft is downed during a flight, the chances of its being found quickly are increased dramatically if a flight plan is on file. An aircraft flight plan includes the type and color of the plane, the total number of "souls on board," the airport from which the flight originated, the destination, the time of departure, the estimated flight time, and the total amount of "fuel on board" measured in hours and minutes.*

# 3

# FLIGHT PLANNING

The last three bits of data described above are all time-critical. The time of departure, estimated flight time, and amount of fuel are the main reason pilots file flight plans, because they are the basis of beginning a search-and-rescue operation. While the Federal Aviation Administration (FAA) encourages pilots to file plans for all flights, there is no requirement to do so when the weather permits flying by Visual Flight Rules (VFR). Nevertheless, most good pilots file flight plans regardless of the weather.

If FAA personnel know from the flight plan that an aircraft took off at 1:00 P.M., was estimating a flight of one and a half hours and had three hours and forty-five minutes of fuel on board, then they have two important pieces of information about that flight. First, they can expect to hear from the pilot shortly after 2:30 P.M., the time the flight was due to arrive. Second, they know that the aircraft must have landed somewhere by 4:45 P.M., the time the fuel would have run out.

When an aircraft is overdue, the FAA first checks with the tower of the destination airport. Often, the pilot arrived on time, but neglected to alert the FAA to "cancel" the flight plan.

However, if FAA staff find that the aircraft has not arrived as scheduled at its destination, they will call other airports along the filed route of flight to see if the pilot was forced to stop short of the destination. Exploratory calls of this nature continue until the fuel exhaustion time has passed. At that point, the search efforts become more intense because it is certain that the aircraft has to be on the ground somewhere.

Filing a flight plan, even in good weather, also serves as an aid to the pilot by reinforcing exactly how long the aircraft can remain aloft with the fuel on board.

When an aircraft flight is expected to enter clouds, a flight plan becomes a prerequisite. Flying by Instrument Flight Rules (IFR) requires information that is more specific. For example, a pilot flying in clear weather may choose any altitude and may change it at will during the flight. However, in the clouds, because of the lack of visibility, the altitude becomes critical, and it is assigned by, and cannot be changed without coordinating through, air traffic controllers.

## DON'T GROUND YOUR FLIGHT PLAN FOR LIVING

If you want to be a fair-weather flier in life, then you only need a VFR flight plan. If you don't want to be grounded in life by the small obstacles that appear daily, then you have to do the extra planning required to fly in instrument conditions.

Checking weather reports and forecasts is one of the most important aspects of flight planning. However, no one interprets the weather. Rather, the information is presented in a standard format for all pilots. You will never read in a weather report, "Today, in Chicago, the fog is too bad to fly." Instead, you would obtain the straight facts on Chicago's morning weather: "Ceiling indefinite, two hundred overcast, visibility one-half mile."

Airport weather reports are never interpreted because, depending on the pilot's abilities and the capabilities of the aircraft, they can mean different things in different situations. The Chicago

*35*

weather report has unique implications for pilots of small aircraft and for pilots of jetliners. It describes a ragged, low-hanging cloud ceiling averaging about two hundred feet above the ground and visibility in fog of only one-half mile. Most private pilots would know automatically that the conditions require an instrument flight for which they are not rated; that report would spell the end of their flight planning until the skies cleared.

On the other hand, if that same Chicago report were read by instrument-rated private pilots of small aircraft, they could plan a flight, but would have to consider many more factors than if the skies were clear. For example, the ceiling and visibility might be too low for one aircraft yet be safe for another, or the specific equipment in the plane might determine whether an instrument approach was legal or possible.

Even if the private pilot could legally depart with the given conditions, the weather would have to be updated continually as the flight progressed. Complete safety would depend upon constant vigilance to ensure that the pilot could handle the changing conditions.

The very same Chicago weather report would have a completely different effect on a jet airline captain. A jet pilot might peer down at the report over his reading glasses while sipping a cup of coffee, then casually look up at the operations agent behind the weather counter and say, "Put an extra two thousand pounds of fuel on board. Detroit will be our alternate." Then, folding up the papers, the pilot would head for the departure gate with no further thoughts about the weather.

As the flight progressed, the captain would have the co-pilot recheck the Chicago weather when they were about thirty minutes away from landing. If the updated report revealed that conditions had deteriorated dramatically and the ceiling and visibility were less than that stated in the original report, it would merely mean they would fly a different approach into Chicago. Visibility and ceiling conditions that can prevent a modern jet airliner from landing are quite rare, though the most well-equipped jet can be grounded by particularly bad weather.

## *SOMETIMES YOU'VE GOT TO SAY "NO"*

Companies — and individuals, too — should be aware of the current condition of the economy before taking on additional financial burdens. Some people want to plod forward regardless, even though the handwriting is on the wall — and maybe even the ceiling and the door — that now is not the time.

The all-time example of ignoring the conditions may well have occurred with the space shuttle Challenger. It had been delayed several times before and NASA was feeling pressure to get the show on the road. It was as if NASA had decided, "Look, this is starting to get embarrassing, let's go ahead and launch," even though they were not ready under the conditions at launch time. The Challenger disaster had an especially profound impact on me.

Ever since I was in grade school and saw Alan Shepard on television blasting off into space, I was fascinated by the idea of flight and space travel. When Shepard was launched from Cape Canaveral, Florida, I made a promise to myself that one day I would see a rocket ship blast off. As I got older, I came close several times. Finally, a few years ago, I had a speaking engagement in Florida, so I checked to see if there were any shuttle launches scheduled. There was a shuttle on the pad preparing for blast-off, but my schedule didn't permit me to be in position at launch time. As it turned out, they kept postponing the launch while I continued to work. There were five or six cancellations.

Finally, when my job was completed, I had some time to spare and the launch was scheduled for the next day. So, I took a chance and drove down to Cape Kennedy, hoping to be there for the one that would go.

I'll never forget how cold it was. There was ice on the water, even in Florida. I was so surprised, thinking to myself, "This is freezing!" The next morning, with an air of anticipation built over more than twenty-five years of my life, I drove to the launch site.

The cold must have kept people away. Although I did not arrive early, I found a parking place across from the launch pad where

I would have a perfect view. I could see with my naked eye the spaceship sitting on its pad.

I can still remember the incredible, awe-inspiring excitement I felt when those shuttle engines came to life. My whole body trembled, yet I no longer felt cold. As Challenger rose from the pad, I thought to myself, "That spaceship has a teacher on board. My wife, Beverly, is a teacher and I know she would love to be on board." My wife shares much of my love for flight and I was sorry she was missing the sight of this launch.

Then I thought how much I would have liked to be on that shuttle myself. I don't know how many times in my life I have dreamed I might one day fly in space. So many things raced through my head. If NASA would let me fly in a shuttle, I could be a spokesman for the space program, traveling all over the country and inspiring people about travel in space. I mentally projected myself up there with that crew, trying to imagine what they were feeling and how the earth would look from the window of a space shuttle blasting off.

About a minute after lift-off, I heard a sonic boom and was amazed that, as far away as the shuttle was, I could hear the first and second stages separate. Then it became clear that what I had heard wasn't a sonic boom. After all the years of waiting, the first space launch I witnessed was the Challenger exploding in midair.

## SOMETIMES A DELAY CAN BE POSITIVE

There is a clear lesson in the shuttle story for all of us who intend to map out a flight plan for living. Shuttle space flights are the most intensely planned flights that ever take place. Nonetheless, any flight plan, no matter how well devised, sometimes requires alteration. Occasionally, you have to recognize that you simply cannot get to your destination and that what seems like a passive response — delaying the trip — may be the most positive action you can take. Get-There-itis can be a fatal disease.

As in flying, most delay-causing conditions in life are usually short-lived. Maybe you need to clear the fog from your own mind about something. Maybe having the wisdom to delay will actually produce an unexpected gain.

## *SAYING "NO" UNDER PRESSURE*

As the pilot of an executive jet in the VIP transport unit at Andrews Air Force Base in Washington, D.C., my friend Ron Wagner regularly carried some of the most important, powerful, and influential people in the world. The day that this story took place, Ron, while still a lieutenant, was scheduled to carry a four-star general from Andrews to Scott Air Force Base near St. Louis. Normally, a flight transporting a four-star general would have been commanded by a higher-ranking officer, but Ron was one of the top pilots in his unit and was regularly tapped for the highest-level missions.

This particular four-star general was the commander-in-chief of the Military Airlift Command (MAC). He was responsible for all the transport aircraft in the entire United States Air Force. In effect, he *owned* the aircraft Ron would fly, and their scheduled destination was the general's headquarters. Further, this general had a reputation for being red-hot-tempered.

It was a beautiful spring day when Ron showed up for the flight. The entire base was on alert for every move the general made and the weather briefers had prepared the necessary papers well in advance, expecting Ron's arrival.

Ron says he clearly remembers that the first thing he saw was a big red circle smack on top of Scott AFB depicting an intense low-pressure area centered on St. Louis. Springtime and deep low-pressure centers usually combine to produce some of the deadliest flying weather, often spawning tornadoes in that part of the country. Ron made his decision almost instantly, having no doubt that his aircraft was not flying into that weather, four stars or not.

If he needed any reminders that his decision would be scrutinized by the highest-ranking officers in the Air Force, his beliefs were reinforced when the major behind the weather desk handed him a stack of photocopies of the complete weather briefing package. He looked across at Ron and said, "I figured you'd be needing these, so I made extra copies."

Ron went to a bank of phones and called the command post to say that the flight would not depart as planned. The major who answered the phone was aghast at what he heard. "Lieutenant, do you realize what you are doing by canceling a flight with General Carlton on board? You can't do that!" He calmly replied, "Sir, I just did." When he hung up the phone, Ron turned and saw that the chief pilot of his unit was standing behind him, had heard every word, but said nothing.

Waiting for his head to roll, Ron returned to the weather desk. Within two minutes, Ron's operation officer, a full colonel who was also responsible for Air Force One, charged into the room and ran to the weather desk. He slid to a stop in front of Ron and said, "You must be Lieutenant Wagner." "Yessir," Ron replied as he handed over one of the extra flight planning packets.

This colonel was a stereotype of the rugged, strong-willed military commander. He stood in front of Ron chomping nervously on a fat cigar, looking like George Kennedy in the original *Airport* movie. In less than a minute, he looked up at Ron and said, "Well, I wouldn't go either, but I sure as hell wish you would!" Then he popped Ron in the shoulder with his big fist and said, "Just kidding, Lieutenant." He grabbed a few more of the weather packets and vanished into the VIP waiting room where the general was waiting. Ron noticed that his chief pilot was still in the room, observing everything, and that he had now been joined by their squadron commander.

Though Ron knew he had made the correct decision — the thunderstorms didn't care one whit about four-star generals — he left the base concerned that he might be hanged so that other officers could get off the hook with the general. When Ron walked into his squadron's offices the next day, he was not surprised to find he had been scheduled for an early morning meeting with his commander and the chief pilot.

No one but the commander knew it yet, but the chief pilot had been ordered to transfer to another unit, creating an opening in the chief pilot's office. They had considered Ron for the job, and what they saw the day before confirmed their decision. The cigar-chewing operations officer was particularly impressed and wholeheartedly agreed.

As it turned out, when Ron left the base after canceling the flight, the entire staff at MAC headquarters held vigil over the weather at Scott AFB. Within twenty minutes of the scheduled flight's arrival time, a tornado ripped through a neighborhood two miles from the base. Ron assumed his new duties as a chief pilot in the Presidential Wing in Washington, D.C., on the day his promotion to captain became effective.

Who would have guessed that canceling a flight would propel Ron into the position of flying planes for six U.S. presidents and countless foreign and American dignitaries? Ron's story seems to prove that sometimes discretion is, indeed, the better part of valor.

## YOUR FLIGHT PLAN IS A STATEMENT

I had a great dad who was exceptionally involved in my young life. He always told me that he wanted me to do two things. The first was to become an Eagle Scout, and the second was to get a college degree. I had great respect for my dad and great respect also for these two goals. I filed my flight plan for both of those destinations with Dad, he helped me in every way he could, and I accomplished both of them.

Dad was a positive influence in my life in almost every way except one. He was not fulfilled by what he did for a living and seemed to live for the day when his work would be over. He was employed in the same job for forty-one years, hating it and always knowing exactly how long he had until his retirement. He never grew personally and never moved on; he simply plugged away at the same old miserable job.

Because he took his obligations to his family and children so seriously, he worried that he would fail at anything new. Although he stayed at his job for the security it provided, to me it

*41*

seemed a great example of what I *didn't* want in life.

After I finished college and had worked for years at what my dad would call a "real job," I quit to become a professional speaker. I didn't have much in savings, so it was a real leap of faith. My wife had a job, but it wasn't enough to last us long if I failed completely. Soon, Dad asked me some details about my work.

"What kind of retirement do you have?"

"Dad, I don't have a retirement plan."

"What kind of salary do you have?"

"Dad, I don't have a salary."

"Son, you need to go back to your steady job, get a salary and build up your retirement."

Nevertheless, I kept on speaking and struggling and, about a year later, Dad again asked, "Son, when are you going to get a real job?"

Dad could not believe I would leave a good job at a big, established company to go out on my own. He couldn't understand how I could leave the "security" of the corporate salary and the retirement. Though the job I left was fabulous, I knew it wasn't right for me.

I tried my best to explain it to Dad. Still, he couldn't believe I would walk out on my security, and he asked me again, "When are you going to get a real job?"

This time I answered, "A real job? You mean one that I can hate all the time and count the days until retirement? So I can hate getting up in the mornings because I have to go to work? Is that the kind of job you mean?"

Then I realized that there are differences in filing a flight plan for living and a real aviation flight plan. In aviation, you can only file with the Federal Aviation Administration. In life, you can choose with whom you file. Dad had been a great help with my flight plan to become an Eagle Scout and to earn a college degree, but he was not the best person with whom to file my flight plan for professional speaking.

People change throughout the various stages of life. As you

change, remain aware of those with whom you can entrust your flight plan for living. File it with those who are the most committed to seeing you arrive at your destination and who will not try to alter your plan to suit a destination they might have chosen instead.

## FLYING TOGETHER

Football in Texas is not like anywhere else. For many Texans, football is the whole reason for being, and boys start playing as early as the fourth grade. Many Texas parents would give anything to have their sons play on a state championship team.

When I was in the sixth grade, nearly everyone on my football team was a Boy Scout and my dad was our Scout leader. It had come to the point in our season when we needed to win one more game to win the conference and to be able to play for the state championship.

The Boy Scout troop had planned an overnight campout, which turned out to be scheduled for the night before the critical football game. Because there was not much sleeping done at these overnights, the parents of the Boy Scouts on our team kept their sons at home to avoid risking the state title to a bunch of exhausted boys.

Despite what the other parents did, my dad believed I could do both. "Patrick," Dad said, "you're the only player on the team who's going on the overnight. A lot of other parents think you won't play well enough because you'll be too tired after camping out. Since I'm the Scout leader I want you on the campout. But, Patrick, because so many parents are mad at me, I want you to show them you can do both things. When we get back tomorrow from the overnight, I want you to win the game for me." My father had never asked me to win a game for him before.

Though it was only a short-term goal, I felt powerful because I had a flight plan for that weekend and I knew that Dad was there to hold the vision with me. Because of the power of our joint plan, I put out my best effort. I played with reckless abandon, we won

*43*

the game 14-0, and I scored both of our touchdowns.

Better yet, we went on to the state championships, where I was the captain of the team and won that game, too. I'll never forget that last regular-season game, though, because Dad asked me to win it for him.

When we share a plan with people we love and we are encouraged by them, we can reach down inside and put out extra effort. It's truly amazing how much extra energy we can find to push back our limits because we are sharing it with people who care.

## FLYING SOLO

We won't always be able to file a flight plan with a loved one. Sometimes there won't be anybody with whom to file. That's when the self-encourager in us comes into power. Even if you do get to share your flight plan with someone else, you are the only one who can fly your own plane. So, even if you don't share your flight plan with another person, it can always be on file with someone you love a lot — you!

When I was playing football at the University of Oklahoma, one of my teammates was Eddie Hinton. We both played the same position, but Eddie was a better athlete. He became a first-round choice in the National Football League draft during our senior year, and started his rookie year for the Baltimore Colts. Today, twenty years later, he still holds the record for the most receptions at Oklahoma University.

During our freshman year, Eddie played behind me for a while, because he wasn't trying his best at first. Then Eddie, who had been the Oklahoma high school player of the year the previous season, filed a flight plan with himself. He decided he wanted to be great, so he set about using all his potential and went on to be a great All-American college player, college record-holder, and NFL professional.

Eddie's flight plan did not stop with football, which is why he was a winner then and he's a winner today, going on to excel in business when his football career ended.

Of course, there was lots more to Eddie than merely wanting to be great. Filing a plan that he had not been prepared to fly would have been pure folly. Eddie prepared himself with a lot of training and a lot of preflight planning. With this solid background, he had a reasonable expectation of reaching his destination safely.

*A pilot's license differs from an automobile operator's license in one major respect. To keep a pilot's license in force, an individual pilot is required to have regular medical examinations and check flights. This is called maintaining currency.*

# 4
# ARE YOU CURRENT?

There are four levels of pilot's licenses: student, private, commercial, and airline transport. A student aviation license will be issued to anyone who passes a medical examination. The license entitles the student to take lessons with a flight instructor and, when authorized by the instructor, to fly an airplane solo. However, students cannot carry passengers until they earn a private license.

A commercial license is required to fly anyone or anything for hire. The airline transport pilot rating is the Ph.D. of aviation and entitles the holder to fly large aircraft and operate scheduled commercial flights.

Before being qualified to fly in instrument conditions, a pilot must have had recent experience flying a certain number of practice approaches. Commercial and airline pilots must maintain their currency requirements separately for every type of aircraft they fly.

All of us need to have current knowledge and experience before we can be assured of reaching our destinations safely. However, there is no legal requirement in most fields to update training, so there are many people who go for long periods without maintaining currency.

Some doctors, for example, may go for years without learning new techniques, because they can practice medicine legally without continual checks on their competence. I have met teachers, also, who have been teaching for twenty years without taking a single course beyond their original requirements. From what I know of some of them, I'd say they've really been teaching the same year twenty times.

## NO ONE OUTGROWS THE NEED FOR TRAINING

Some pilots may fly the same airplane for twenty years, but they return to school regularly to learn the latest about aircraft changes and to hone their skills. Even the most seasoned pilots note that they have learned something new after completing a current training course.

The currency requirements in the airline industry are complex. Captains are required to return to the training center twice annually either for school or for a checkride, and they must also renew their medical certificates every six months. It is illegal for captains to fly passengers on jetliners without successfully completing their six-month check requirements.

In addition to their checkrides and medical examinations, all pilots must take an annual ground school refresher course on aircraft systems, weather phenomena, Federal Aviation Regulations, company regulations, and security procedures. First officers (co-pilots) and second officers (flight engineers) must have annual checkrides and physicals, too.

### Green and Growin' or Ripe and Rotten

The airlines can teach us a lot about continuing to stay current and growing as we fly through life. We cannot spend our entire lives cruising on autopilot. Sometimes, we've got to come down out of the clouds, shoot some approaches, and make some landings to remain practiced and proficient. Even if everything has been going smoothly, we can never tell when we'll have to deal with unexpected adverse conditions. Or, as my wife is fond of saying, "You're either green and growing or ripe and rotten."

I have always taken a professional attitude toward my flight duties in the private planes I have flown. I've always sought instruction in new planes and kept my flying skills current. Nonetheless, there are still times when routine assumptions about our currency are not enough.

I was engaged to speak in Hot Springs, Arkansas, and decided I was going to fly there. When I got to the airport, the plane I usually flew was in pieces all over the hangar.

When I asked what was going on, the shop owner told me that my plane was down for its one-hundred-hour check. "But don't worry," he said. "I've made arrangements for you to fly another plane over to Hot Springs. It's just like yours except that it's five years newer."

"Okay," I said, and went out to start my normal preflight checks.

The replacement was brand-new, with only six flight hours on it. I completed my checks and departed for Hot Springs, which was about a two-hour flight. I landed safely, gave my speech, and went back to the airport at about eleven o'clock that night.

The weather for my return trip wasn't bad, but it was starting to mist fairly heavily. Because of the mist and the fact that the airplane was parked in a dark area of the airport, I did something I don't usually do. I didn't have a flashlight so that I could see to complete my preflight check, so I said to myself, "It flew in, it'll fly out."

*Preflighting by Assumption*

In pilot talk, this is known as "kicking the tires and lighting the fires." When I started out, I had taken on plenty of fuel for six hours of flying. Since it took two hours to get to Hot Springs, I decided it should take two hours going back, and I thought I would be in good shape.

After I took off I suddenly encountered some fairly heavy rain. I got on the instruments and rechecked everything thoroughly. That was when I noticed that my gas gauges read almost empty. Let me tell you, flying at midnight, in a rainstorm over southeastern Oklahoma and nearly out of fuel, is not a good situation.

Feverishly, I dug out my charts to find the nearest airport so I could land pronto. I soon discovered Broken Bow International in Oklahoma. It wasn't much, but when I broke through the clouds and saw the lights of Broken Bow, it looked like the world's greatest airport to me.

I landed, parked near the fuel shack, and got out to see if I could find anyone to fuel my plane. It was raining so hard that I was soaked by the time I sprinted into the shack. Inside, I found a sign that read, "After ten o'clock, if you need fuel, call this number. . . ."

There was a pay phone in the corner. I went over to use it, stuck my hand in my pocket and came up with a total of eight cents in change. I had more than a hundred dollars in my wallet, and back then it only took a dime to make a call, but none of that paper money was going to do me any good.

At that point I had two choices: I could hang out in the shack until the airport opened at seven in the morning, or I could hike down to the airport operator's house, which, according to a map in the shack, was about a quarter mile down the road. There wasn't anyplace in the shack to lie down, not even an old couch, so I decided to wake up the airport operator.

When I stepped out of the shack and onto the road behind it, my boot sank into nothing but mud. The only way to get to the operator's house was to take a dirt road in the pouring rain. I was wearing a brand-new pair of expensive boots, a recent gift from my wife, but I wanted to leave Broken Bow that night, so I pressed on.

I sloshed through mud up to my ankles, disgusted with myself because it was all my fault. If I had done what I was supposed to do in Hot Springs, I would have been starting my descent into Dallas instead of ruining my new boots.

The airport director was a model of southern hospitality and

*49*

was happy to come out and fuel my plane. He drove me to the shack, brought the fuel truck around, and within minutes was yelling in to me, "What do you want me to do about these auxiliary tanks?"

My mind flashed and I asked, "What auxiliary tanks? My plane doesn't have auxiliary tanks."

About that time, he yelled again, "Oh, never mind, they're already full."

That was when I remembered that, though it appeared the same as the one I usually fly, this airplane was newer and had a different fuel system. Because I was not current in that particular plane, I didn't know it had auxiliary tanks and didn't know how to put them into use. I could have crashed with all that fuel on board.

I learned two lessons from this experience. First, I was reminded of the importance of staying current with the equipment you use so you can tap the hidden reserves when you need them. In this situation, I could have crashed due to what I thought was fuel starvation, and burned up because of the fuel in the auxiliary tanks that I didn't know were there.

Second, we all get into pickles as a result of things that are our own fault. In this case, I assumed I was current because the newer airplane appeared identical to mine. Anytime you upgrade to a new model of anything, you can be sure that something has changed. Keeping up with the changes will help you get maximum efficiency out of whatever you do, and may even prevent a disaster.

Have you thought lately about how you might tap your hidden reserves? Would you know how to "throw the switch" even if you wanted to use your reserves?

## LEGAL DOESN'T ALWAYS MEAN SAFE

Sometimes maintaining currency can be a matter of personal integrity rather than legality. Pilots have died in crashes that occurred during flights for which they were perfectly legal. However, legal and safe are often two completely different things.

One snowy January afternoon a few years ago, Washington's National Airport experienced the tragedy of its first crash in more than thirty-two years. At first, many people blamed the airport itself because it has short runways and is located close to downtown Washington. However, when the final reports were in, there was only the crew to blame.

The crash of Air Florida's Flight 90 into Washington's 14th Street bridge gripped the entire Washington area. Yet, the whole event was merely one mistake by a couple of inexperienced guys who simply screwed up. Both pilots held legal ratings to fly that plane, but neither had ever flown a jet airliner in the snow. That crash — flown by a crew that was legal, but not safe — resulted in many deaths, severe injuries, and a psychological blow to thousands of people throughout the region.

The factors that caused the Air Florida crash can also be observed in fields other than aviation. It takes more than a piece of paper earned in school to determine whether individuals are qualified to reach their destination. One should ask honestly, as the Air Florida pilots should have asked, "Am I truly qualified for this flight?" Your immediate physical survival may not hang in the balance, but the survival of your physical, financial, and emotional happiness may.

## ARE YOU LEGAL TO CONTINUE?

When pilots begin a flight, unless they've completely miscalculated, they will have enough fuel on board to reach their destination. However, once under way, the wise pilot will continually recheck the winds, the ground speed, and the weather at the destination. A flight begun legally and safely can easily become illegal or unsafe because of changed conditions.

Each flight should start with enough fuel, and continue with constantly updated conditions to ensure that reserves remain sufficient in case of bad weather. We can update as we fly by reading newspapers and books, listening to audio tape programs, seeking the counsel of mentors, networking with others in like situations, attending career and life-orientation seminars, and taking care of ourselves physically.

A good time to gather updates is when you are cruising and things are going well. Many people use the smooth flight times to sit and stare blankly at whatever scenery passes by, watching television, for instance. The cruising times are when good pilots call Flight Service — catch up on professional journals, calculate financial needs, or learn new business techniques.

## WHAT KIND OF FUEL DO YOU USE?

There are many kinds of aircraft fuel, and they each serve a different purpose. An aircraft fuel company in Dallas was responsible for refueling the small piston engine planes of a local commuter airline. One day, an employee of the fuel company accidentally filled some of the piston planes' fuel tanks with jet fuel. The next commuter plane that took off had enough of the right kind of fuel in the bottom of its tanks and in its fuel lines to taxi out and take off. Once it was airborne and the jet fuel reached the engines, the plane crashed.

Just as there are many kinds of aircraft fuel, there also are many kinds of human fuel. In addition to the obvious detrimental effects of drugs and alcohol, it's amazing the effect that a poor diet can have on your body.

An Air Force pilot friend of mine found out the hard way what junk food can do. He was stuck in a temporary duty assignment away from his home base in a hostile winter climate. The weather was so bad that he didn't want to walk far to eat, so every night he had a hamburger and french fries at a pub in the basement of the building where he was staying.

After three weeks of this diet, he took an Air Force flight physical. The next day, he was called in by the flight surgeon and told that he had not passed his physical.

"It doesn't make sense to me," the flight surgeon said. "All these years, you've had perfect physicals and now this. Have you changed your diet lately?"

When my friend told him about the burgers and fries, the doctor said, "I'm sending you back to your home base. I want you to eat properly for a week and then have your blood work redone." One week later, after eating plenty of vegetables and other healthful foods, the laboratory report on his blood was back to normal.

If the right fuel is not going into your tank, you may be terribly short of what you need to energize your flight.


## THE HYPER-KEY

All my life I've been a sports car aficionado, yet I've never had a new one, or even a nice one, until recently. I finally bought myself a new Corvette from one of my clients, Mike Beaver of Beaver Chevrolet in Dallas.

Mike is a self-made millionaire who dropped out of high school to get into the car business. Later, he realized that he needed a college education, so he put himself through college and now has one of the largest Chevrolet dealerships in Texas. To stay on top, Mike realizes he must continually strive to get better, and he has invited me several times to speak to his employees. Mike and I became friends because he is a great self-encourager.

I got a call from Mike not long after he sold me the beautiful sports car that he said I needed to help me encourage myself. He said, "Patrick, you've got to come out here and drive a new car I just got in." Though I had barely driven my last new car, I knew Mike well and if he said I needed to see this car, I believed him. So, I drove out to his dealership and sitting right in front was a bright red, brand-new model of the Corvette, the ZR-1. The ZR-1 is a special racing version of the Corvette that sells for $70,000, and Mike's dealership is allocated only one per year.

The ZR-1 looks like a regular Corvette on the outside, but there is a huge engine under the hood. I couldn't believe how fabulous it looked. It had a beautiful red leather interior, a six-speed manual transmission, and every accessory I'd ever dreamed about.

Mike put me behind the wheel, climbed into the passenger side, and told me to fire it up. Within minutes, I had pulled out onto one of the interstates in Dallas. Mike looked at me with a grin and said, "Step on it!"

It was a magnificent ride. I couldn't believe a car could be so fast; I had never imagined anything like the ZR-1.

After a short drive, I turned back toward the dealership and finally came to the ramp for our exit. When I got off Mike said, "Stop for a minute." I did, and when I looked over at him he had that silly grin on his face, and he said, "How did you like that?"

I stuttered and tried to come up with something to express how impressed I was. I hadn't come down to earth enough yet to be eloquent, but he got the message that it was everything I had ever hoped for in a car. The only thing I remember was saying that I couldn't believe a car could be so fast.

*Tapping the Invisible Reserve*

Mike's grin widened and he reached into his pocket and pulled out another key. "Patrick," he said as he stuck a key into a second slot on the dash, "this is the hyper-key. Without this key turned on, the ZR-1's engine is limited to only about 60 percent of its total power potential." As he turned the key, his grin grew again and he said, "Now you've got its full power, let's go around again!"

My fantasies had been fulfilled during the first trip, using only 60 percent of the power. I could hardly imagine what it would be like at 100 percent, but the second trip was even more spectacular than the first. Mike later told me that the ZR-1 is the fastest mass-produced car in the world.

This story is a good illustration of the value of being current about the equipment you use. I could have driven that car a long time without knowing about the hyper-key.

Moreover, a lot of us are like the Corvette ZR-1. We normally only use a fraction of our power, keeping our full potential locked out. We need to use our personal hyper-key to tap our hidden powers.

*Finding Your Own Hyper-Key*

No two of us will have exactly the same hyper-key. My hyper-key would not tap the locked away power in your ZR-1 and vice versa. Only you can know exactly how to unlock your own hyper-power, which is why self-encouragement is so important. If you depend on other people for your encouragment, they may never use the right key for your inner power source.

It's easy to enjoy your jaunt through life, just as I appreciated the first drive in the ZR-1. We may even be impressed with what we can do. However, regardless of how impressively we may be performing, we've all got a hyper-key that will make us more powerful.

What is your hyper-key? What do you need to tap your hidden inner power? Are you current with yourself physically and mentally so that you will be able to make the most out of your hyper-key when you do switch it on? Once you know you are qualified and current, you can go out to the airplane on the ramp and begin your preflight checks.

*The preflight phase can be broken down into two distinct parts. The first part, flight planning, is mostly paperwork and is done on the telephone or at a weather counter, as discussed in chapter 3. Once that is complete, the pilot proceeds to the aircraft and begins the second phase of the preflight. This involves ensuring that the plane is physically able to complete the planned flight safely.*

# 5

## PREFLIGHT CHECKS

Several factors go into determining if an aircraft is ready to fly, and one of the most important is a check of the plane's mechanical condition. Each aircraft has a maintenance logbook that, when signed by a properly certified mechanic, indicates that the plane is mechanically airworthy. An appropriate signature in the logbook does not mean that the aircraft is in perfect condition. Jet airliners rarely take off in perfect mechanical condition, but the repairs that are needed must not affect safety and must be noted in the aircraft's logbook.

The pilot's main duty with respect to the plane's mechanical condition, then, is to ascertain that the items needing repair will not cause an unacceptable loss of capability for the flight as it is planned.

Certification of airworthiness also is not a statement that the aircraft is legal for all flights. For example, the instrument landing system of an aircraft might be completely inoperative. If the weather at both the departure and the destination airport is clear, the instrument landing equipment is not required because the

56

plane will be airworthy without it. However, if the plane was scheduled to land at Chicago, where a dense fog required an instrument landing, then the aircraft, though mechanically sound in other respects, would not be legal for that flight.

There is much more for a pilot to consider than the mechanical condition of the aircraft and its subsystems. Other critical steps include checking the fuel on board, and checking the oil. The oil in aircraft engines is much more important than the oil in a car's engine. When you're driving, you can pull into any gas station for a quart of oil, but you don't have that luxury in the air. Having enough fuel on board isn't any good if the plane takes off without a full oil tank for each engine.

The early phases of your life are more like driving than flying because, like the corner gas station, you can turn for help to parents, siblings, or teachers whenever you need to do so. Flying is more like going out on your own. It's more difficult to rely on others when you are aloft, and some types of help are impossible to get in-flight.

## WEIGHT AND BALANCE

Every plane has a maximum safe weight at which it can legally take off. Many pilots cheat on this limit, especially among small commuter airlines, because they can increase profits by carrying more passengers or freight.

The other part of the weight and balance factor is that the weight carried by an aircraft must be distributed properly throughout the plane for the aircraft to be controllable in-flight. An airplane may attempt to take off at a weight that is well under its maximum allowable total load, but if too much of the weight is in the tail of the aircraft, it will pitch up and stall out of control.

Every person has a limitation on what they can carry and still operate safely. Sometimes we may take off when we shouldn't because, in airplane terminology, we are overgrossed. An individual may be able to fly overburdened for a long time without any incidents, but will be less able to handle the extra pressure of unforeseen conditions if they suddenly arise.

Maintaining a balance is as important in other aspects of life as it is in flying. Suppose you take on a project that you have plenty of time to accomplish. Then, instead of spreading the work out evenly over the available time, you procrastinate until the last minute and then have to push beyond your limits to complete the project in a last-minute crunch. Properly distributing the work would have kept everything in balance and prevented a breakdown.

### PERCEPTION VERSUS REALITY

I believe that our perceptions create our reality. In the last chapter, I described my experience in a plane that I thought was out of fuel, but that actually had gas in its auxiliary tanks. My perception in that plane was that I was out of fuel, and it became a reality upon which I acted.

Our perception of reality can change in a split second. For example, it took a lot of effort to get fuel into my plane's tanks that night. Had I known about the auxiliary tanks, my perception of reality would have been altered instantly. Yet the reality of the extra fuel on board would have remained the same.

I learned another great lesson about perception from my daughter Alicia's soccer team. I had been Alicia's coach for many years and we were preparing for the first game of a new season. When the players on my team arrived, I expected to see their usual cheerful faces. This time I noticed that they were coming onto the field slowly, their heads were down, and their shoulders were humped over. Clearly, something was wrong with my usually enthusiastic group.

Then I realized that we were about to play a team whose members were all eleven years old, a full year older than the ten-year-old girls on our team. At that age, one year older can mean much bigger physically. Our team had been beaten badly by the older team during the previous season, so I concluded that the low morale on our team was because of last season's loss.

Since encouraging people is what I do for a living, I got the team together and gave them a pep talk, saying everything I could think of to get them excited and to build their confidence level. When I finished, one of the girls on my team looked up at me with a pair of big blue eyes that almost had tears in them and said, "But, Coach, we don't have a chance."

"Of course you've got a chance," I said. "Listen, ladies, you've all grown bigger and stronger and faster since last season. You've practiced a lot more, you've gained more skill, and you can do it!" I even got down on my knee so I could look them all in the eye, doing the best I could to get them fired up with the right mental attitude.

Finally, another little girl looked over at me and said, "Coach, look over there," as she pointed across the field to the other team. "Can't you see that those girls are all wearing *bras?*"

Then it hit me. To a group of ten-year-old girls who didn't wear bras, a group of eleven-year-old girls who wore them seemed completely out of their league. Those undergarments changed my team's perception of themselves and created a fantasy of super athletic powers in their competitors. Their perception was reality to them.

The other team was not a great deal better than my girls, but we lost badly that day anyway. About the only thing that would have made a difference during our pregame huddle was to have handed out bras to my team. Failing that, the game was over before it began. My team lost on the basis of what the other team was wearing.

### PERCEPTION IS REALITY

What *I* was wearing almost got me into trouble once when I first moved back to Dallas. One Saturday morning, I was out mowing my lawn. My neighbor, Nick Russell, who sold cars as an avocation, came over and asked me to ride downtown with him and pick up a car he was ready to sell. Nick assured me that he had finished working on the car, that it was ready to go, and all I would have to do was drive the used car back home.

When we got downtown, I saw that Nick's car was old and that, while he had fixed it up mechanically, it looked like a jalopy.

I jumped in and headed for home. On the way back, I decided to stop at a roadside café for a quick lunch, even though I was a little embarrassed being in that old heap and wearing the ratty clothes I had put on to mow the lawn. I remember thinking that this certainly was not the way I would normally look when I went out to eat.

After lunch, when I got back on the highway, I noticed that police had erected barricades at almost every exit ramp. Then I remembered that former House Speaker Sam Rayburn was reportedly near death and that it had been rumored that President Nixon would fly in to see him one last time. I figured the police had barricaded the roads for security in preparation for the president's arrival.

*My Chance to See the President*

Never having seen a president of the United States in person before, I pulled over to the side of the road hoping his car would drive past. I sat there for a few minutes and, all of a sudden, I heard a loudspeaker blast out, "Get out of the car slowly, put your hands on the roof and do not move!" I looked around and saw that I was surrounded by police with drawn weapons, all pointed at me!

I tried to explain that all I wanted to do was get a glimpse of the president, but several of them rushed forward yelling at me to get my hands on the top of the car, and not to move or talk. Then I was frisked aggressively and the car was searched thoroughly.

While the police were searching me and the car, people who had been in the café where I had lunch began pouring out and screaming, "Get that criminal out of here! He's probably going to try to shoot the president! Stop him!" I was horrified that people who knew nothing about me would yell such things; then I started seeing myself from their perspective.

All they knew was what they saw: a guy who needed a shave,

wearing ratty clothes, driving a beat-up old car. It turned out that the people in the café had seen me stop at the side of the road, and they had called the police.

I thought surely the police would soon realize that I was an innocent citizen. Instead, it got more complicated when the officers who searched the car discovered that it was not mine. To them, this began to look like a criminal scenario, with me driving a stolen car. Fortunately, after asking me a lot of questions, the officer in charge eventually believed my story and told me to get back in the car and leave. You can bet I drove straight back home as quickly as the speed limit allowed.

*Looking Like a Winner*

This was a lesson not only in perception versus reality, but in the power of first impressions. Despite all the suspicion about me on that highway, I knew that I was the same guy who really drove a nice car and wore a three-piece suit. But I didn't look like that person to the people in the café, or to the police. That afternoon, I learned the important lesson that you always have to look like a winner.

Naturally, we cannot look our best all the time, but this story dramatizes what can result from the impression that others get after only a glance at you.

As you preflight yourself or your business for a new flight, pay attention to your perceptions and to the perceptions of others. Are you avoiding a new adventure because you perceive it as being beyond your abilities? Or are you overconfident for reasons that have no basis in reality? Do you judge others by their appearance? How would you be perceived based on what you look like right now? After my experience with the police in Dallas, I never wear anything that I wouldn't be caught dead in!

## DO WHATEVER WORKS BEST FOR YOU

Preflight planning can take on many forms, and what works for one person may not work for another. Whatever you may discover from watching people around you prepare for their destinations in life, you've got to make your preflight suit your own way of doing things.

I once met someone who had a successful preflight technique that would have ruined me. I was scheduled for a television appearance on the Dallas-based Dynamic Achievers World Network (DAWN). Aired early in the morning around the country, DAWN brings in some of the best motivational speakers from around the country to offer people something positive with which to start their day.

The procedure at DAWN is to tape in one sitting the segments of several speakers, each of whom records three or four speeches. Since each taped segment is thirty minutes long, the whole process takes many hours.

Speakers taping at DAWN are allowed to bring in a small audience, and I invited some of my friends. As it turned out, I didn't get started until about ten-thirty that night, so my friends had been sitting there quite a while by the time I began. I was also exhausted because I had flown on an all-night trip from Hawaii, and I had worked all day on the speeches I would do on the show that night.

Though it was late at night when I was introduced, the emcee, Ty Boyd, behaved for the taping as if he were well-rested, bright-eyed, and fresh. I'll never forget that I had to search deep down inside to encourage myself before I could offer an uplifting and peppy "Good morning everybody, welcome to the DAWN show!"

By the time I finished all of my segments, it was after one in the morning. The taping was on a weeknight, so many members of the audience had to rise early the next day to go to work. As for myself, I knew as never before that I would never be a night owl, because this incident was proof positive that I do not function well at night.

As I was leaving the sound stage, I heard some rock music drifting through the building. I stuck my head in the door where it was coming from and saw a rock-and-roll band cranked up and blasting the studio apart. I walked in and asked a guy standing in the back what was going on.

He said, "We're practicing for my tour."

"Oh? What tour is that?" I asked.

He said, "My name is Julian Lennon."

I was fascinated to spend time with the son of a man who had been one of my heroes, the late John Lennon of Beatles fame. Julian told me they were practicing for his first big American tour, and I asked why they were practicing so late at night. I thought that, with his connections, he could have rehearsed any time he wanted and not been relegated to the leftover, late-night time in the back of a television studio sound stage.

Julian told me that he chose the time because the members of his band are all night people, and they practice best late at night. It reminded me of a rock song by another band from his father's era, "Different Strokes for Different Folks," by Sly and The Family Stone.

Here was a guy who knew when his own energy and the energy of his band members were at their highest, and he built his schedule around their optimum. They started rehearsing at one in the morning and were going to play all night long. Julian knew what worked for him, and he was doing his preflights when he would be at his best.

## ARE YOU PREPARING TO FAIL?

When an airliner crashes, the losses are always far higher than expected. Stepping away for a moment from the terrible human tragedy, the destruction of the plane alone creates absolute havoc. There are financial problems in having to replace an airplane that probably was not insured for full replacement value, and there are scheduling problems surrounding the absence of the crashed equipment.

When your failure to prepare causes a crash, the true loss is rarely limited to what is directly observable. The Challenger loss deeply affected the entire nation, yet I never heard anyone say, "Damn, those space shuttles are expensive and we don't have many of them. This is going to hurt our nation's space industry."

*63*

The focus, which was naturally on the human side of the loss, made an entire nation question our ability to maintain quality and exercise good judgment in the space program. The less observable loss in this instance was the damage to the space program itself, a valuable national resource.

None of us goes through life alone. If we are wise, we will tune in to others around us and listen even when we are told things we don't want to hear. Listening anyway, and trying diligently to view our actions from another person's perspective, may broaden our horizons and prevent us from exploding in midair.

*When airborne on a filed flight plan, one of the first things pilots do is contact air traffic control. This activates their flight plan by putting them in contact with controllers who will watch their position on radar, route them away from other aircraft, and allow them to complete your flight safely. Controllers are the traffic cops of the sky.*

# 6

# AIR TRAFFIC CONTROL

None of us is omniscient, so we can't see everything around us all the time. A pilot in a speeding jet might not see another plane that may be obvious to a controller viewing the big picture on radar. It would be easy for a controller viewing it on a radarscope to avert a midair collision when the planes are ten miles apart, but the pilots may not be able to see each other until they are so close that their high rate of speed will grant them too few seconds to avoid tragedy. Similarly, our friends, business associates, and families can see obstacles in our paths that we may miss. As air traffic controllers do for pilots, other people may be able to tell us how to alter direction to avoid potential danger.

## THE PROMETHEAN URGE

There is a Greek fable about a man named Prometheus, from which we have derived a concept known as the Promethean Urge. The idea is that the more capable and confident you are, the greater your urge to take care of things by yourself and not to rely on the input or help of others.

Americans may have the highest collective proportion of people with the Promethean Urge. It probably results from our rugged frontier heritage: the "can do" spirit, the John Wayne macho image.

The Promethean Urge has its place in some areas of life and under certain circumstances. For example, once airborne, a pilot has to have confidence in his ability to land safely because no one is going to drop in and do it for him.

However, none of us has all the answers all the time. There are 240 million people in the United States and more than 5 billion people worldwide. None of us can go through life without interacting with others, so we need air traffic control to warn us of the dangers we cannot always see. Many people in our lives have a better vantage point for some things than we do. To fly through life as smoothly as possible, we've got to let these people in.

This concept seems to fly in the face of much of our popular culture: Sometimes you've got to relinquish control. Most of us have a very hard time doing that, although we can reap tremendous rewards and advantages when we do.

For instance, airline captains do not fly the aircraft all the time, although they did at one time. In the early days of commercial aviation, the captains were treated as demigods and it was said there were only two flight rules that a co-pilot needed to know: "First, the captain is always right, and, second, if you believe the captain is wrong, see Rule One." Now, though, the best captains in the business have a healthy respect for their fellow crew members.

During a typical work sequence in which a crew flies together for three days operating ten separate flight legs, the captain will alternate each leg with the co-pilot. Moreover, on the legs the captain flies, he may relinquish control several times to the co-pilot. The captain may do this to check an instrument approach chart or some maintenance problem with the aircraft, or to eat a meal or go to the lavatory. In any case, the flight is safer and the captain is better able to keep positive control of the overall flight by relinquishing direct, hands-on control at strategic times.

During the strategic moments in life, it may be better if we allow someone else to steer for a while. Just as co-pilots rarely question the captain's ultimate authority, few people will question the control you exercise over your own life, even when you follow their advice or allow them to help with your responsibilities.

To relinquish control, a confident captain must have two essential elements in place. First, the captain must have a broad enough perspective to know he doesn't know everything all the time. Second, the captain must feel certain that the co-pilot is worthy of trust.

At various times in our lives, each of us plays the role of captain or the role of co-pilot. Of course, we will always remain the captain of our own lives, relinquishing control only to update our status or refresh ourselves before resuming our duties. We should also be prepared for the times we will be called upon to serve as co-pilot, respecting the trust granted by those who take our advice or permit us to fly while they enjoy a much needed period to rejuvenate.

## COACHING IN PERSPECTIVE

In addition to sharing our workload with the co-pilots in our lives, there are other people to whom we look for support. These are the flight instructors of our lives, our coaches, those who, formally or informally, provide us with the knowledge we need to fly.

Even the most seasoned airline captains return twice yearly to their company's training centers for refresher courses conducted in flight simulators. Unfortunately, the Promethean Urge, especially in adult American males, creates an ego problem that often precludes additional coaching. The fact is that no one is ever too advanced at anything to refuse additional guidance.

Joe Montana is the epitome of a successful football quarterback. Even if you loathe the San Francisco Forty-niners, you have to admit that Joe Montana is the best at his craft today. If anyone who has ever played the game had a right to act on his Promethean Urge, it would probably be Montana.

Yet Montana freely accepts coaching from a man he does not particularly like. Why? Because he is professional enough to know the secret about coaching: The coach does not have to be better than you, he only needs a different perspective.

A quarterback cannot see the overall game from his position on the field. He cannot see the patterns of all the defenders over the onrushing defensive linemen and, even if he were tall enough to see over them all, he would only be able to focus on one area of the field during a play. The coach on the sidelines, on the other hand, has the ability to see things that the quarterback cannot. It's not because he's better, but because he has a better perspective.

To enhance his perspective, the coach on the sidelines is in constant contact by phone with team spotters in the booths high atop the stadium. These spotters see each play from an even larger perspective. Moreover, the spotters have the advantage of instant replay from a variety of angles and elevations. Just as the sideline coach can see more than the quarterback, the spotters can see more than the sideline coach.

When we accept advice from a coach, we are showing our intelligence and our understanding that one set of eyes and one set of ears cannot possibly absorb everything. The spotters pass on their most relevant observations. The coach sums up the information from all of his spotters, filters it, blends it with his own perspective, and sends in a play to the quarterback. The judgment of the quarterback is not eliminated by this system because only the quarterback can decide which receiver should get his throw, and that decision can only be made from the quarterback's perspective.

In flying, you will never hear a captain refuse to obey a controller who frantically advises the pilot to "turn and descend immediately!" Sometimes if you take the time to question the validity of the coaching advice, the moment has passed and the instructions are no longer of value. Don't allow your Promethean Urge to cause you to refuse coaching.

If you do not already have a mentor or coach in your life, open yourself to finding people you trust. Once you decide to accept someone's coaching, accept it and don't second-guess everything they say. None of us will ever play the great game of life alone.

## PLAYING IN TUNE WITH THE BAND

Although we could much more easily learn to fly an airplane if we did not share the skies with anyone else, that luxury was available to only two people in history, Orville and Wilbur Wright. Since then all fliers have had to learn the rules of the air so they could safely share the skies with other pilots. Today, the skies are so crowded that the rules of sharing take more time to learn than the mechanics of flying. We need to work in concert with the people around us.

I have wanted to play a guitar since I was a kid in grade school, but I was dyslexic, so I couldn't read music. Worse, I was tone-deaf, so I was unable to learn to play by ear. By the time I got to high school I decided to attempt to learn anyway, so I got a friend to teach me some chords and I finally learned to do a bit of strumming.

It wasn't long before some friends and I decided to form a band. Rock bands generally have two guitar players, the lead guitar and the rhythm guitar. It was my ambition to play lead guitar, because I thought of myself as a lead guitar kind of guy.

A friend of mine played lead guitar in another band, and I used to go to his house and watch him play. There was one song in particular that I liked and especially wanted to learn how to play well. I watched my friend play it over and over, carefully watching exactly where he put his fingers. Then I went home and practiced doing exactly what he did, and I'll never forget how elated I was when it finally came together for me.

During the next rehearsal with my own band, I told the guys that I had mastered this song and I wanted the whole band to practice it. As we started practicing, although I was doing exactly what I had watched my friend do, my playing sounded terrible.

I soon discovered why: I had learned the song in the key of G and the rest of the band was playing it in the key of A. We were all doing exactly the right thing, but we didn't mesh.

We may learn how to do something perfectly while we're alone, but we don't live alone and we have to be able to play in the same key as those around us. In this case, there was no way for me to adjust my playing because I was merely imitating the pattern that matched my friend's. Fortunately, the rest of the band had more musical talent and they adjusted to me. Once we were playing in the same key, the song sounded beautiful, but I could only do the lead on that one song and only in that one key.

Most pilots learn to fly at small uncongested airports. Later, after they have mastered the mechanical principles of operating the airplane, their instructors will have them practice at a busy, crowded airport. There is nothing wrong with focusing on the mechanics of learning how to do something, of course, but eventually we have to learn to fly in traffic.

In fact, learning in solitude can be a powerful tool to prepare you for the rigors of the real thing. When my friend Mark first began playing basketball regularly, he could only dribble with his right hand. More accurately, he *could* dribble with his left hand, but not with anybody guarding him and certainly not well enough to get through traffic in a game.

Mark wanted to learn how to drive forward for a lay-up dribbling with either hand. He tried to practice the move by himself but found that he didn't even know which foot to lead off from as he pressed forward toward the basket for the score. Finally, Mark got the perfect formula from a highly skilled teammate.

Mark's friend showed him the steps to follow, then told him to stick strips of tape to the floor exactly where his feet needed to go during the drive to the basket. Mark was told to drive in repeatedly for the score by stepping on the tape strips until the proper placement became second nature. By practicing this way, Mark eventually was able to make the move in traffic while being guarded. He now *owns* that maneuver and is equally deadly from either side.

## NOBODY'S PERFECT

Coaching can be an extraordinary asset to our lives, but no coach should be viewed as infallible. After my freshman-year football season at the University of Oklahoma, our coach was fired and replaced by Jim McKenzie from the University of Alabama. McKenzie brought the Alabama philosophy of lean and mean to the Sooners of Oklahoma. At the time, my "in shape" playing weight was 196 pounds, but McKenzie put each of us on the scale and told us how much weight we had to lose. With his coaching, my weight went from 196 to 185. As a team, we lost a total of four thousand pounds.

The next year, we were beaten terribly when we played Notre Dame. They had a team of giant players that year, who were every bit as quick as we were and outweighed us by an average of forty pounds each. It quickly became obvious that McKenzie's philosophy of lean and mean was not working. While his method had worked well at the University of Alabama, the Sooners had a different playing style and game plan; lean and mean did not serve us well.

However, the lean and mean philosophy did come with a silver lining. One of my Sooner teammates was the great Granville Liggins. Granny, as we called him, was a star player, an All-American who was a huge man. The coach thought Granny was overweight and laid down an ultimatum that no player was exempt from making his target weight. Granny had a harder time than most, and on weigh-in day he had fallen short of his goal.

The coach pulled him from practice and said, "You go out and run and don't stop until you've made your weight goal." I'll never forget the picture of our All-American star running back and forth across the practice area. He was dragging like he was nearly dead, but he didn't stop.

The rest of us knew that if the coach would do that to Granny, then we'd all better make our weight, and we all did. That's the silver lining. The coach proved his credibility by setting a goal that everyone was required to follow, even our All-American.

*71*

From then on, everyone on the team respected the coach's statements, knowing that he meant them and that he would enforce them.

Lean and mean may not have been the right principle for the Sooners, but the coach showed us he would not tolerate a double standard. It has been easier for me in everything I've done since then to uphold my standards with integrity. Seeing what he did has helped me many times to avoid compromising my standards, even when it might have served a short-term goal if I had.

## COACHING IS WHEREVER YOU FIND IT

I have found coaching in some of the least likely places and during times when I wasn't even thinking about it. One of the ways I seek coaching or flight instruction is to get out and visit the heart of the cities in which I have speaking engagements. I like to meet the people and see what makes the town tick, what factors make it unique. It's one of the greatest benefits of my profession.

Not long ago, I was speaking in Chattanooga, Tennessee. Being a Civil War buff, I wanted to visit Lookout Mountain outside of Chattanooga, a site where a great Civil War battle was fought. I wanted to walk the grounds and see exactly what the soldiers in that great battle saw. I wanted to see how the battle had taken shape, how the commanders maneuvered and what they hoped to accomplish by taking Lookout Mountain.

I rented a car and drove out to Lookout Mountain for an afternoon. On the way out to the site, I saw a great big sign that said, "See Ruby Falls." I thought that sounded interesting; after all, you only go around once and I didn't want to miss something terrific.

As I got closer there was another sign, "Don't Miss Ruby Falls," which made me decide that I should stop to see it. I thought once again about the Lookout Mountain battlefield that was my original destination, but decided to follow my intuition and accept the coaching of the roadside signs.

Soon I saw yet another sign that said, "This is it. Ruby Falls. Turn in here!" Well, I was already hooked and I simply turned in.

I parked, went into the office, and bought a ticket.

A tour guide took a group of us into an elevator that went deep inside Lookout Mountain, nearly down to its base. When we got to the bottom, we left the elevator and the tour guide started us through a little crevice that went way back inside the mountain. We walked a long way through a narrow and winding passageway until the tour guide stopped us and asked us all to hold hands. Once she saw that we had all joined hands, she turned out the lights.

*The Inner Beauty*

With all the lights out — in total blackness — she continued to lead us through the passageway. We moved slowly, literally snaking our way through the narrow corridor. As we rounded a corner, we began to hear the sound of cascading water. It was frightening as we got closer and the sound of the rushing water got louder and louder. I wanted desperately to see where I was going, but this was obviously one of those times when I had to rely on the direction of my coach.

Suddenly, she turned on the lights and we instantly beheld one of the most beautiful sights I have ever seen: Ruby Falls. It is the largest known enclosed waterfall in the world, where the water cascades down for more than 190 feet in a stunningly beautiful setting.

Ruby Falls was discovered by accident. Someone was drilling a water well and the drill broke through the ground into a large underground opening. The drillers searched for an opening to the cave that they now knew was inside Lookout Mountain. When they found one, they took torches and went inside to explore.

I tried to imagine their surprise when they first saw by the light of their torches what would come to be known as Ruby Falls. I suspected they were awed by the knowledge that they were the first people ever to set eyes on this spectacular sight. I also thought about their good fortune in finding the cave. If they had been drilling a couple of feet either way from the place where their drill broke through, the drill would have remained in solid rock and

73

they never would have made the discovery. It amazed me how such a beautiful treasure was found by the lucky placement of a drilling rig.

*Finding* Your *Ruby Falls?*

Standing inside Lookout Mountain, I realized that we all have a Ruby Falls inside of us, a beauty as wondrous as Ruby Falls waiting to be found. Like the drillers who discovered Ruby Falls, we have to be brave enough to illuminate our insides and explore for our own internal beauty. If the drillers' fear had kept them outside the cave, the world might still not know about its largest enclosed waterfall.

Searching for your Ruby Falls might be picking up a book like this one, but don't lose heart if you don't find it quickly. Remember how close the Ruby Falls drilling crew came to missing their discovery. If you merely skimmed this book, hitting a couple of chapters that sound interesting to you, you might skip the part that would help you most and never know that you had missed it.

If you don't discover Ruby Falls by yourself, you may be able to come close by following the coaching of someone you trust. I had to follow that tour guide faithfully, in the dark, through a narrow and frightening passageway. If I had resisted and demanded to see Ruby Falls in a way that would have made me more comfortable, I would not have had the chance to see it leap out of the darkness the way it did for those first brave explorers.

## YOU CAN BE A COACH, TOO

Many of us narrowly miss much of the beauty in life by rushing past the people we pass daily. How many of them have a Ruby Falls deep inside that could bless us in ways we never imagined? How many of them could discover their Ruby Falls if you cared enough to take their hand in the dark and lead them down a path with which you are familiar? Just as we amass benefits from those who coach us, there is much to be gained by serving others when they ask for our help.

As you go through life, keep an eye out for signposts leading to out-of-the-way places like Ruby Falls. The day I discovered Ruby Falls, I could easily have driven past it because my mission was to walk the battlefields on top of Lookout Mountain. Instead, I ended up someplace I never dreamed existed and it added more to my life than I had expected to get from seeing the battlefield. Be careful that you are not rushing past the hidden beauty in the people and the places you see every day.

None of us spend our entire lives being coached or coaching others. Sometimes we get to punch on the autopilot and kick back and relax. While we all need those times in our lives, there are ways to get the most out of them, improving the flight by maintaining awareness of the big picture, and enjoying the scenery while avoiding complacency.

*The time spent en route is normally the easiest part of a flight, giving the pilot a chance to relax and enjoy the view. One of the first things that most pilots do when they level off en route is to engage the autopilot, which flies the plane at cruising altitude, freeing the pilot to monitor aircraft systems and navigational instruments, to put away the charts that were used for departure, and to prepare the maps and charts required for the approach and landing.*

# 7

# EN ROUTE FLYING

While flying on autopilot is the most restful phase of flying an aircraft, a good pilot will not allow it to become an excuse for lax behavior. This is when a check is made of the weather ahead, when speed is calculated, and when the fuel consumption is monitored to ensure that it is going according to the flight-planned schedule. The free time on autopilot could lull one into a false sense of security and result in an unexpectedly tough situation that could have been prevented by a bit of routine vigilance.

### WATCH FOR THE SUBTLE SIGNALS

My Air Force pilot friend, Ron, was once in command of a training flight with two student pilots. They were practicing nighttime, cross-country flying on a mission that had been planned for one student to fly to another airport, shoot some approaches, then trade seats with the other pilot for the same maneuvers on the trip to home base.

During the quiet of the outbound cruising portion of the flight, Ron noticed a tiny hint of an unusual vibration. He asked the other pilots if they heard anything but, being new to the aircraft, they did not perceive the vibrations and noises as unusual. Continuing to listen, Ron thought he recognized the sound of a bearing going bad in a piece of electrical equipment. Though the noise increased, the students were unable to detect anything that sounded ominous.

Upon arrival at the destination airport, Ron let the first pilot fly his approaches. Then, they swapped seats as planned and the second pilot flew his approaches. By this time, the noise seemed obviously louder to Ron; he was sure the bearing was about to fail and they would soon experience an electrical malfunction. Still, neither of the students noticed anything awry.

Since it was a night flight, Ron did not want to leave the area of the airport, especially since the bearing could be replaced quickly if he landed where he was. If he had an electrical problem en route, he thought, he might be forced to divert to an unplanned base. So, Ron instructed the second student to fly a couple of extra approaches and, within a few minutes, a light appeared on the aircraft's electrical warning panel alerting them to the failure Ron suspected. Since they had remained in the local aircraft pattern, they landed uneventfully from the next practice approach, the part was replaced, and they returned home safely with only minimal delay.

Avoiding serious problems in life can often come from being attuned to those subtle disturbances that let you know that something may not be quite right. You may be able to escape having to make snap decisions, and evade serious disruptions to your plans, if you observe and act on the things you pick up during the quiet, cruising times in your life.

## USING AUTOPILOT

A lot of people go through life on autopilot all the time because it's so easy. This is completely different from a planned rest during which you allow a co-pilot to reduce your workload in-flight. Some people abuse the benefits that the autopilot times provide and try to operate forever without effort. In other words, many people engage their autopilots and disengage their brains, and they waste their cruising time.

Autopilots are terrific labor-saving devices but like most of the computers in our lives, they will faithfully do whatever we program them to do and nothing more. If you tell your autopilot to cruise straight ahead while you lie back and go to sleep, it will do exactly that. If a mountain were to loom ahead, the automatic pilot would fly you perfectly straight and level right into it. Or if you ignored your fuel gauges, the autopilot wouldn't care; that's not its job. Autopilots have more than once flown planes right up to the instant the engines quit from fuel starvation.

Even if you are on autopilot for a while in your life, never forget that you — and only you — are in command, that you are ultimately responsible for the safety of the flight and those who may be riding along with you. The passengers in your life may be your friends, your family, your co-workers, or an entire company. If you are a doctor, the passengers could be patients who are betting their lives that you will use your autopilot cruising time wisely.

A pilot may disengage the autopilot to fly the plane manually around a storm that develops unexpectedly along the planned route. Without the vigilance that warns the pilot of the changing conditions, the autopilot could be permitted to fly straight into a thunderstorm that could tear the aircraft apart and toss it right out of the sky. There are times in our lives when we must be ready to take control.

### TRIMMING YOUR LIFE

Not all airplanes have autopilots, but even the smallest aircraft have a feature known as the trim control. The trim control is used to balance the aerodynamic forces on the plane, so that the pilot need not make continuous input to the controls.

If the aircraft is out of trim, the pilot must hold a constant and steady pressure on the controls even to cruise in level flight. Holding that pressure will quickly exhaust a pilot. Under some conditions, it may require control inputs that exceed the pilot's physical strength. Trim is not a single setting that you make and leave; it changes as fuel is burned and different speeds change the pressures the airstream places on the wings. When an airplane is trimmed properly, its control pressures are balanced so that when the pilot releases the controls, the plane will maintain its attitude.

Flying a plane in trim is like driving a car with perfectly aligned front wheels on a level road and letting go of the wheel. If your front wheels were out of alignment and you took your hands off the steering wheel even for a second, the car would veer off the road. That's like flying a plane out of trim.

You can trim your life so that little input is needed, even without an autopilot. For example, you may have adjusted years ago to balance perfectly with your marriage partner. As the years go by, your partner will change. If you leave the trim setting where it was when your flight began, you will find the setting that once served you now has the aircraft in a slow descent. If you do not readjust the trim, you will have to expend constant physical energy to arrest the descent.

You will soon tire of constant pressure, and when we are tired, most of us get irritable and are easily provoked. You may then find yourself always at odds with someone with whom you thought you had a balanced relationship. Worse, you might not make changes either to the trim or to the control forces, and the airplane will continue its descent until it crashes.

If it seems that your spouse is not the person you married, you're probably right. Your spouse may not be going through life at the same speed as when you last set your trim to an even balance. After all, throughout a flight, an aircraft's center of gravity changes, requiring continual trim adjustments. Your own conditions change constantly, too.

The company you work for is probably not the company with which you started years ago. It, too, must evolve or it would not survive long. The changes are necessary for our health and survival. So, instead of complaining about the changes, a pilot simply makes adjustments as needed to meet changing conditions.

Many people go through life out of trim. Often, they get fatigued and complain that life is difficult. With small alterations, they can usually smooth out their lives. We cannot avoid aspects of our flight through life that take effort, but staying in trim makes it easier for us to make the manual control inputs we need.

However, you cannot fly an aircraft by trim alone, a mistake that many new pilots make. This would be like people who change location constantly, or who end up in a long string of marriages and divorces, in an effort to eliminate all the stress in life, never willing to fly even a short distance with pressure.

If you go to your job every day complaining that you hate it, then you need to reset your trim. Either change jobs or make a conscious decision to stay in your job and quit complaining. If you decide to stay in your job, perhaps you can find a way to trim out the pressures, some of which may be self-induced.

Changing trim to balance the forces is not restricted to your personal life. Your company may be flying out of trim with its market environment, causing you and everyone else to hold constant pressure to keep it from crashing.

During the time I worked for IBM, the company was forced by changing markets and increasing competition in the computer industry to switch from selling computers to selling services. A layer of management was eliminated and the whole philosophy of its marketing was changed to help its customers and meet their needs. In effect, IBM adjusted its trim control so that the corporation would automatically maintain its attitude.

If a monolithic, nearly monopolistic corporation, with hundreds of thousands of employees, can make such dramatic changes, you, too, can make trim adjustments. In the quarter following these changes, IBM had a $2.5 billion increase in sales, the second largest in its history. This is a good example of the saying, "Doing what you've always done will get you where it's always gotten you. To move on, move on!" In other words, trim constantly.

## ENJOY THE SCENERY

While you are using your cruising time wisely and keeping your trim in proper balance, you've also got to take time out to enjoy the view from your lofty perch. Caution is wise; too much caution can paralyze us so that we're never able to see the forest for the trees.

When I was growing up, I always wanted a cashmere sweater, but I never gave myself permission to enjoy owning one. I suppose it showed a lack of self-esteem, because I felt I didn't deserve the luxury.

One Christmas several years ago my mother asked me, "If you could have anything for Christmas you wanted, what would it be?" I told her how long I had wanted a cashmere sweater and, on Christmas morning, she came through for me and I finally owned a beautiful, white, V-neck, cashmere sweater.

I was so pleased with it, I put it in a box and stored it on the top shelf in my closet. I looked at it occasionally because it was so beautiful, but I never wore it because I was afraid something would happen to it.

In Dallas, where I live, there are not many days cold enough to wear a cashmere sweater, and soon the weather was too warm to wear it that season. Though it remained on the shelf throughout the summer, I never forgot about it.

On the first cold day of the following winter, I decided that it was time to wear my sweater. I went to the closet, took it down, and carefully opened the box. To my complete horror, I found that it had been eaten full of holes by moths.

Here was something I had wanted for most of my life. I finally got it and only used it as an incubator for a family of moths. It was like flying on a beautiful day and only focusing on the instruments inside the plane.

Everything we have is going to be food for moths eventually, or trash in a landfill. The true value in anything is in using it. Our treasures are better when they are shared with others; a treasure has far less value if it sits on a shelf, hidden away in a box. Many people would have admired my cashmere sweater, and would have enjoyed watching me wear it. Instead, I spent all my cruising time worrying about what might go wrong with my elegant sweater. What was I waiting for, my next life?

We don't have to subscribe to the philosophy of instant gratification to enjoy the scenery in our lives every day. There are things most of us truly want and deserve, but feel that we have not earned. When will we be worthy? What will it take? It's only a thing anyway; wear your cashmere sweaters.

It may not always be easy to enjoy the scenery. I'll bet there have been times in your life when you felt as if it took all your energy merely to stay even, that when you have looked out the window of your life, it seemed as if you were flying backward. Does that sound familiar? It can happen in life. It can even happen in flying!

## FLYING BACKWARD

I made the decision to become an airline pilot while I was working at another full-time job. I had flown in the military, but I needed to log more flight hours and get current experience to be more competitive for an airline job. The only way for me to do that was to work during the day and fly whatever I could at night.

The first paid job I had was flying a small airplane that had a lighted billboard attached to the bottom. You have probably seen something similar on the side of the Goodyear blimp or outside your local bank. A computer inside the plane controlled a grid of lights hung under the plane to make messages scroll across the billboard. The company that owned the plane sold advertising space on the billboard and programmed the advertisers' messages into the computer. I flew the plane around town at night so people could see the advertisement in the sky.

The plane was old and not powerful, and the addition of the apparatus that held all those lights underneath increased the drag considerably. I knew even then that it was dangerous, but I felt it was safe enough, so I took a chance. My instructions were to fly

*82*

as slowly as possible so that the people on the ground would have time to read the full message as it scrolled across under my plane.

One windy night, after I turned on the message and slowed the plane to its minimum safe speed, I looked outside and saw what looked like the ground below moving backward. I was flying more slowly than the wind into which I was heading, and the net result gave me a negative ground speed.

Have you ever had a similar experience, when you were doing something only for the money and felt yourself going backward? If it's happening now, ask yourself, "What am I doing now that I might later look back on and say, 'I can't believe I did that just for the money'?"

I would never do anything like flying that little billboard plane again, but when you are new to something, you may take risks you wouldn't otherwise take. Anytime you find yourself doing something only for the money, you are only taking care of today. Move on to what you truly want to do, so that you can also take care of tomorrow.

Let me guess, your response to that is "But I've got to have the money right now." Or maybe it's "I *need* this job now, I'll do something better *someday.*" I don't agree with that philosophy. In my experience, when you do what you love, money will follow.

If you were able to get the job you're doing, you can get another. If you've got yourself in a box, you also can get yourself out of it. When I quit my full-time job to become a professional speaker, it was, for a while, a financial setback similar to being grounded temporarily. At least I was not up in the night sky making money and flying backward in my life. Once I began to be successful at speaking professionally, I was headed toward a destination I wanted and I flew there with greater enthusiasm than I had for any of the jobs I ever took simply for the money.

## IT DOES *GET BETTER THAN THIS*

I always listen with annoyance to the commercial for a particular brand of beer, because the last line says, "It doesn't get any better than this." It drives me crazy to hear that because it's not true. I also listen with dismay to people who say, "If things got any better, I couldn't stand it," and to another commercial for a brand of painkiller whose slogan is "Life has gotten tougher, so we made our aspirin stronger."

It can always get better than this! The only thing about life that never changes is that life always changes. Remember the famous line from *Gone With the Wind,* "After all, tomorrow is another day." So, if every day is going to be different — if life is going to evolve daily for each of us and never stay the same — then only one of two things can happen: it's got to get worse or it's got to get better.

The aspirin commercial promotes the twisted belief that life has changed for the worse and that it's perfectly normal to need a drug to get through it. This reiterates the same underlying philosophy that life isn't going to get any better, so you'd better have a large bottle of aspirin handy.

Our true mission in life isn't our destination, it's the journey. No destination you choose will be the end of the line in your life any more than one destination is the end of the line for an airline pilot. Instead, view each of your destinations as refueling bases or checkpoints to fly on toward your next dream.

As self-encouragers, we need to inspire ourselves with the knowledge that tomorrow can always be better than today. If we accept statements such as the one I cited from the beer and aspirin commercials, we send our subconscious a message that will be hard to overcome. Read all the self-help books you want, but if you accept the thought that it can't get any better and it's so bad that you need drugs, then you are wasting your time.

This philosophy of taking an aspirin because things are tough today is what some experts have called *reactive-responsive* behavior. People who are reactive-responsive see each day as a series of problems to overcome and lack a vision of what they want to have in the future. Taking care of problems all the time can easily be headache-producing, so it makes sense that these people believe they should rely on aspirins to get through life.

The kind of philosophy that addresses a much higher part of ourselves is one in which we see each day as an opportunity to create our vision of what we want most. Remember our discussion about destinations: create a vision in your mind of the destinations you most want to see and then see yourself already there. However, if your perception is that this is as good as it gets and that you will need an aspirin to get through tomorrow, your perception will be your reality and that is exactly what you will create as you fly through your life.

*If you've envied pilots because they seem to have the luxury of avoiding curves and detours, you've been wrong. The highways in the sky are sometimes as crooked as those on the ground. It has only been because of recent high-tech breakthroughs that pilots have been able to proceed "as the crow flies."*

# 8
# GOING DIRECT

The aircraft navigation system in this country took shape as a strange, crazy-quilt, patchwork arrangement. You've probably seen the same type of growth pattern in your roads. Roads in the nation's highway system that were laid out before advanced construction techniques permitted using the most direct routes have now evolved into circuitous major thoroughfares. No one driving them today can understand why all the twists and turns are in the road.

The construction of our long-range aviation navigation system was driven by the same political forces that shaped the routes of many of our highways. The core of the system was built around a series of radio stations, called VORs (very high frequency omni ranges), emitting a signal to a receiver in an aircraft that determines the plane's distance and direction from any of the stations.

If an airport has a VOR station located on the field, it is easy for a pilot to locate. In the early days of aviation, politicians lobbied hard to get stations built on their airports, and the proliferation of them also was enhanced by their relatively short range, which restricts most airways to no more than 130 miles between stations.

So, we needed a lot of stations and every city with an airport wanted one.

Once the stations began to blossom, the en route navigation system was constructed as a web of highways in the air, connected by thousands of VOR stations. As you can imagine, there is no combination of cities that lies in a perfectly straight route between, for example, Chicago and New York at intervals of less than 130 miles. The result was that for a pilot to fly between two distant cities, he had to navigate in a series of zigzags, cutting back and forth to fly over the cities that were most closely aligned with the planned route.

In the early 1970s, three factors came together to improve the patchwork nature of air navigation. First, computer miniaturization gave aircraft radio manufacturers the ability to add a computer to their aircraft VOR receivers that straightened out the kinks in the road. Second, improvements in the computers and radar equipment used by air traffic controllers gave them the flexibility to track aircraft that wanted to "make up their own direct route." Finally, the fuel crisis at that time gave airlines and aircraft owners the economic incentive to invest in updated equipment, because direct routing promised significant fuel savings.

These three factors combined to create an aviation system known as *area navigation,* or *RNAV.* RNAV permitted pilots to fly the most direct route between any two cities in the country, with no further need to pass directly over a series of VOR stations.

We can often find the same kind of improvements in life. Where previously we may have had to travel a zigzag course to get to a destination, we may now be able to take a direct route, saving time, money, and precious, irreplaceable national resources.

This is not to say that the old methods were no good. What we consider "old" today were vast improvements over what *they* replaced. When the VORs were first introduced, they were such a dramatic advancement over what had gone before that they were hailed as magical marvels. Never before had a pilot been able to twist a couple of knobs and get an instant bearing and distance

*87*

from nearby airports. Before VORs, many pilots got lost and ran out of fuel without ever being able to locate an airport. Once the VOR system was in place, as crude as it seems by today's standards, any pilot could locate an airport quickly and land safely.

Nevertheless, we can't stay attached to old ways of doing things. Improvements are a constant part of our lives and they are happening at an ever-increasing rate.

## THE FASTER THINGS CHANGE, THE FASTER THEY CHANGE

A story about the Voyager II spacecraft is a good illustration of how rapidly the world is changing and how important it is to remain current.

The Voyager II, while steadily hurtling through space, has sent us data and pictures from Saturn, Uranus, and Neptune. Voyager's home base is the Jet Propulsion Laboratory in Pasadena, California. The scientists there have to "spoon feed" flight plan information to Voyager in tiny increments because the six computers on board have a total memory capacity of only 32K of RAM. That's less than 5 percent of what the average desktop computer has today.

Why was this high-tech Voyager sent out on such a historic mission with so little memory? Because when it left earth in 1977, today's personal computers were only a dream. Back then, handheld calculators were considered leading-edge technology. When Voyager was launched, we had not yet heard of video cassette recorders, Nintendo games, compact-disc audio players, or the Reagan presidency.

As technology increases, we will all find more and more ways to "go direct" to the destinations we choose in our lives. But I am going to share with you several stories about ways to fly direct, and a couple of stories that may inspire you when you would like to go direct but cannot.

## THE DALLAS COUNTRY CLUB

When I was in the eighth grade, I realized that if I wanted any spending money, I would have to earn it myself. At the time, I lived near the Dallas Country Club, so I went there, introduced myself to the golf pro, and told him I wanted to be a caddie.

He said, "Well, that's fine, but all our caddies are black."

I said it didn't matter to me, and I pressed my case further by telling him that I came in second in the Dallas Open when I was twelve years old, so I was quite a proficient golfer and I understood the game. All I asked for was a chance.

The pro agreed to let me try, so I went out to the caddie shack. Since I was the first caddie at the Dallas Country Club who wasn't black, I had to prove myself. My first problem arose when I was "up" to take the first round.

Two "toughs" approached and said they were going to run me off because I wasn't a black guy and they didn't want me working around their club. Clearly, I was a threat to the natural order of things as they saw it. I told them, "I'm going to stay here and I doubt that you guys can run me off." With that, one of them pushed me and I grabbed him and said, "If you want to start something, you've picked on the wrong guy!" When they realized that I wasn't going to back down, they left me alone and I commanded their respect. From then on, nobody else bothered me, and I remained as the only white caddie at the Dallas Country Club.

That job was interesting because I got to see how it felt to have people try to run you off simply because of your skin color. Some people call this reverse discrimination, but I see that discrimination based solely on one's skin color is never right; it makes no difference which color is on which side of the fence.

At the Dallas Country Club I also discovered a way to make use of my creativity. At the end of the day, many of the golfers went to the clubhouse to clean up, then they had to walk a considerable distance to the lot where their cars were parked. I asked the pro if I could rent a golf cart and make it available free to any of the members who wanted a ride to their cars. When the day was done and the other caddies had gone home, I hung out at the clubhouse in my rented cart, offering rides to those who came out.

Once I got them to their cars, I received a nice tip. I was providing a service that had never existed before, so it made me feel good and it made them feel good because the ride was "free."

## A LESSON IN NEW ORLEANS

I had been speaking in New Orleans and, after my speech, I was out sampling the considerable local flavor of the town. I was in the heart of the French Quarter, walking down Bourbon Street, when a boy came up to me and offered me a free shine. I looked down at my boots and saw that they did need a shine. How could I pass up a free one? Besides, I wanted to find out what his gimmick was.

That kid gave me one of the best shines I have ever seen. I couldn't believe what a beautiful job he had done. Then I remembered my golf cart gambit, when I had offered free rides. I figured I understood — his trick was to do such a spectacular job that he was assured of getting a nice tip.

When he finished with the first boot, I stuck my other boot on his stand and the kid said, "Oh, no. Only one boot is free. The second boot is five dollars." He had done such a good job on the first boot that I couldn't go around with my boots looking that different, so I paid him what he asked.

It was a shame, because I probably would have tipped him five dollars if he had done the second one free, too. Thus, instead of leaving me with a happy feeling that I had done something nice for a kid who truly deserved it, he left me feeling cheated and angry. Obviously, there are many ways of going direct, but when I fly a direct, shortcut route, I prefer never to do it at the expense of others.

## TAKING A HANDS-ON APPROACH

I once filed my own direct, shortcut flight plan to get over a phobia. For as long as I could remember, I had been afraid of snakes. I couldn't explain it and I don't know why it happened — they had simply been something that terrified me.

When I became an officer in the Army, I realized that there was a good chance I would end up in the jungles of Vietnam, where they had all kinds of snakes, and I knew I needed to get that phobia under control. I could see myself marching through the jungle leading a bunch of men and all of a sudden screaming, "Oh, my, a snake!" That would have been a real good way to lose all my credibility and authority right there.

I had read that to overcome a fear, one should do the very thing that causes the fear. So, the summer before my senior year in college, I ended up working for an oil company at a job that involved a lot of driving around on dirt roads in the backwoods between oil wells. On those roads, there were plenty of huge, fat bullsnakes, which are nasty-looking but basically harmless. The bullsnakes would lie out on the warm dirt roads to sun themselves, so I saw them all the time.

One day, I said to myself, "You know, Patrick, you'd better get over this fear of snakes." One day, I saw a snake sunning itself and I stopped the truck. I checked it out from a distance to make sure it was only a harmless bullsnake and though it was, it was also about five feet long and several inches around — about the diameter of a tennis ball. I walked over to get close to it and watched it for a while. Then I got a stick and played with it a little bit and it tried to get away. I wouldn't let it run off because I wanted to show it I was in charge of it and that it wasn't going to intimidate me.

Finally, after five or ten minutes, the snake was getting tired of my little game and was acting sluggish. I was feeling pretty confident and I thought, "You know, that snake is not going to bite me. I'm going to pick it up." So I reached down to grab it the way I had seen people handle rattlesnakes. I worked my way around behind

*91*

it as if I were a real pro and it was a deadly rattler, and I suddenly grabbed it right behind the head and held it up.

At about the same second that I was congratulating myself on my courage, I realized that I hadn't grabbed it close enough to the head. That big bullsnake turned back on me and bit my hand!

Though the snake was nonpoisonous, it scared me to death and I threw it way up in the air. It didn't even draw blood, but it was the thought that I had been bitten by the thing I feared the most.

As soon as the snake landed, I looked at it and was disgusted with myself. I was terrified, but I could see that the snake was as scared as I was. I thought I might never get over my fear if I left then, so I checked myself out and then went back over to the snake.

Though it was trying its best to get away from me, I sneaked up behind it for the second time and grabbed it. This time I did it right, clasping it up close behind its head. I held that snake up and looked it right in the eyes and told it, "You are mine. You are not going to scare, intimidate, or control me." After a few more moments of savoring my victory over my fears, I put it down gently and watched it crawl away.

You've got to overcome your fears logically and in a controlled manner. When you confront them, do it gradually, and don't ever forget that self-encouragers never let fear stop them.

### WHAT ABOUT THE TIMES YOU CAN'T GET CLEARED DIRECT?

Flying direct is often only an illusion. In reality, even a plane that appears to be flying direct is off course about 95 percent of the time. The pilot, or the autopilot, makes hundreds or thousands of small corrections throughout the flight. If the pilot quit making adjustments halfway through a long flight and simply remained on a steady heading, the plane probably would miss the destination airport by many miles.

*A Lesson from Nature*

The caterpillar of a species of silkworm found in North America spins its cocoons among the branches of bushes and trees. The cocoons remain there through the winter months until the transformed crecopia moth emerges the next spring.

The cocoon breaks open to reveal a beautiful brown, orange, and gold moth within it, slowly struggling to free itself from its prison. If an observer were to view this scene, he might feel tempted to slit the cocoon to free the moth more quickly and alleviate the poor moth's arduous struggle.

However, what the observer would not know is that there is a higher purpose in the struggle of the crecopia moth to emerge from its cocoon. As the moth labors to free itself, it pushes its wings against the sides of the cocoon. The pressure of this action forces blood into the wing muscles, strengthening them in the process.

Without that slow, step-by-step process, the moth would emerge with weak, shriveled wings, unable to fly. It would then be easy prey for a hungry predator, and the crippled moth would not likely survive even its first day of freedom.

Many times there is a higher purpose for our slow, sequential struggle. That's when we should remember the crecopia moth. When you face life's struggles, look upon them as helping to make you stronger.

*Persistence Pays Off*

When you cannot go direct, you've got to tap your inner resources for persistence. You will usually be richly rewarded.

Miss America of 1989, Debbye Turner, is an inspiring example of tenacity and self-confidence. Debbye is from Arkansas. She had entered the Miss Arkansas contest and lost it three times, including the 1988 event in which she was considered the favorite to take the top honor. Even her father, usually highly supportive, thought enough was enough, and discouraged her from continuing. Despite those setbacks, she believed in herself and persisted.

Debbye finally won the Missouri state pageant in 1989, when she was studying veterinary medicine there, and she went on to win the top title of Miss America. Debbye has said, "If I had quit when I was sixteen after losing my first pageant, I wouldn't be here today. If I had quit after my third try in Arkansas, I still would not be here today."

Persistence on the level applied by Debbye Turner can help us get through the most trying times in our lives. Even those times that we would call emergencies can become valuable learning situations that we can draw strength from in other endeavors for the rest of our lives.

*There generally is an emergency checklist that the pilot has been trained to use in case of an in-flight emergency. For example, if a pilot loses an engine, the "engine failure" checklist would be consulted. Checklists are written by design engineers, who combine their expertise with that of the test pilots during the development phase of each aircraft.*

# 9
## EMERGENCY PROCEDURES

As we have noted earlier, flying is simple. It's the unexpected that requires skill. In fact, it has often been said that flying is really hours of boredom punctuated by moments of sheer terror.

If the correct checklist is accurately completed, few aircraft emergencies place the pilot or passengers in imminent danger. Most aircraft systems have backups that permit safe landing at a nearby airport. However, if the pilot does not correctly switch to the backup systems or does not make an orderly transition to an emergency mode, the problem may progress to a more serious point.

A good illustration of this is found in one of the emergency checklists for a three-engine jetliner, the Boeing 727. The most critical safety failure that can occur in the 727 is losing both its number one and number two engines, leaving it to fly only on number three. Engine number three is the only one that does not drive a hydraulic pump, so if three is the only remaining engine, the pilot is faced with two major problems. First, the three-engine aircraft must be flown on only one engine and, second, the serious hydraulic failure prohibits normal extension of the landing gear and wing flaps. It would be impossible for the pilot to reach an airport without following proper checklist procedures.

The careful planning behind the 727 single-engine checklist is intended to turn certain disaster into a neatly choreographed maneuver that is a source of great pride to pilots. Since this situation is so obviously life-threatening, every airline practices these emergency operations repeatedly in their simulators. To be certified to fly a Boeing 727, all crews have to demonstrate they can handle this emergency checklist properly.

Similarly, there are few situations in life that have not been handled by countless thousands, perhaps millions, of people before us. Many excellent books, programs, and groups are available today that provide checklists for getting through the emergencies in our lives. We would be foolish to ignore the expertise of those who have been there in order to invent our own checklist while flying along in a crippled aircraft.

The captain of the United DC-10 that crashed in Sioux City, Iowa, did invent his own checklist when he experienced a failure that no one had ever considered to be possible. But he and his crew ended up at the White House receiving a special citation for extraordinary airmanship. Even that heroic crew probably would have traded all the acclaim for a good checklist in-flight.

## WRITE YOUR OWN EMERGENCY CHECKLISTS

While you will not be able to practice the emergencies in your life with the realism of today's jet aircraft simulators, you can get some practice nonetheless. You can buy or update your health insurance, medical insurance, life insurance, or car insurance. You can talk to your family about and practice escaping from your house in the event of a fire. You can update or prepare a will, which will include lining up guardians for your children and selecting someone to be your executor. These are only starting points; you will be able to think of others that apply specifically to your own life.

Many people are superstitious about planning for emergencies, feeling that doing something about them will somehow make them happen. Some believe that preparing a will means you expect to die soon, for example, or that wearing a car safety belt means you expect to crash today.

There are others among us who do prepare. Some people put dead-bolt locks on their doors without thinking of themselves as pessimists. Planning contingencies for emergency situations does not really make them occur.

In America, we seem to operate on the safety edge most of the time. Many people run to the limits of their credit card maximums with no reserves, and savings are at an all-time low. Financially, our society seems to be held together by trick mirrors in a house of cards.

You remember our discussion about being current. Currency includes not only knowing the limitations of the aircraft you are flying, but its emergency checklists as well. The more advanced your level, the more contingencies you need to plan for. For example, a small, single-engine private aircraft has no automatic oxygen masks because it cannot fly high enough to need them. Are you safe to fly your own life, not only in the good conditions that prevailed at departure, but in poor conditions if an emergency comes up en route?

As your life changes and you take on more responsibility, you need different emergency preparations. For example, at the beginning of a flight taking off in clear weather, a pilot does not need an instrument landing system (ILS), but he should know that the system works because he could fly into instrument conditions later. We may have no need for a life insurance policy or savings when we are single, but it's likely that we will one day need a financial reserve.

Before a flight, no one is going to tap you on the shoulder and say, "Hey, you'd better make sure that your ILS is working." Likewise, in life, there is no "big brother" in the sky who will come down and give you notice that now it's time to buy life insurance. You've got to prepare for some emergencies and contingencies on your own.

## *USE THE CREW CONCEPT*

Most of us do not have to fly solo. Our co-pilot might be a spouse, relative, or close friend who can help us get through emergencies. Airline captains are experts at using their co-pilots to fly the plane while the captain handles the emergency checklist. Any captain who tried to prove how good a pilot he was by handling everything alone would never pass a checkride.

Part of the certification process for captains is demonstrating the proper use of cockpit resources, of which the co-pilot is one. Do you use the cockpit resources in your life or do you try to do it all alone? Captains who earn the most respect among co-pilots are those who have the self-confidence to delegate duties.

Delegating duties in the cockpit not only allows the captain increased concentration on a critical task, but it gets the viewpoint of more than one mind into play. The picture may look different from the other side of the cockpit, or a co-pilot may have a unique perspective through which the same information will lead to a different conclusion.

While it probably is true that an airline captain could fly solo 95 percent of the time, including the co-pilot in ongoing decisions in the cockpit gives the pilot and co-pilot valuable practice at working together. It also ensures that the co-pilot remains proficient at using vital skills.

Many people rarely ask for help from those around them when things are going smoothly. Instead, they wait until things get out of hand before they scream for help. An important part of emergency preparedness may simply be working together under routine conditions with those you may need to rely upon in an emergency.

## *LOOK FOR THE SILVER LINING*

For the last seven years, I have spoken at the headquarters of Lockheed Corporation in Los Angeles four times annually. After that many trips to Los Angeles, I've got it all down to a routine.

I take the same flight, go to the same rental car counter, and take the same Highway 405 to the same hotel located near where I am to speak.

One trip, though, didn't go quite like any of the others. It began when I got to the rental car counter and was told they were out of the four-door, automatic, mid-sized sedan I customarily rent. In fact, the only car they had left was a hot-rod, five-speed Shelby Cobra. Though I had not driven a five-speed in several years, I decided to take the car, thinking it might be fun.

Before I left the lot, I remembered the person at the counter said there was construction on Highway 405 and that I needed to take an alternate route. I removed my safety belt, reached over to the glove compartment to get the map, checked to make sure it was the map I needed, and pulled out in the direction of Highway 405.

I saw immediately that my usual access to Highway 405 was blocked by the construction and that I would have to turn around. As I did, I went back under a bridge and found a temporary entrance. Approaching Highway 405, I noticed that one lane was completely backed up all the way and another lane was wide open. I dropped into second gear and pulled into the open lane, easily sailing past the long line of stopped cars. Without delay, I was headed north on Highway 405, back on my usual route.

It was rush hour then and the traffic was crushing. Looking back in my mirror, I saw — way back in the distance — some flashing red lights. Then I saw it was a police car working its way through the traffic. I kept watching the police car as it worked its way past more and more of the traffic, curious to see whom they were after. Finally, the cruiser approached my car and the officer gave me the pull-over signal.

My first reaction was that someone thought I was in a stolen car. "I'll show them the rental car papers," I thought, "and I'll be on my way." I had little time to spare because I was headed directly to my speaking engagement.

Once I stopped, the officer yelled over her speaker system, "Get out of the car and don't move!" When I got out, she came toward me with her hand on her weapon. Though she hadn't drawn it, the look in her eyes made me think she was ready to blow me away and ask questions later.

When she determined that I was unarmed and not wanted for a crime, she said, "You know why I pulled you over, don't you?" I told her that I believed she assumed the car was stolen and handed her my papers to prove it was a rental.

She said, "No, that's not it. You got on the highway in a car pool lane." Well, I had no idea what she meant, and she explained that there is one lane reserved for cars with three or more people in them and "You got in that lane!"

I said, "I didn't see any sign, and besides it was a temporary entrance near all the construction."

"Well, everybody in California knows that this is a car pool lane."

"Oh, but I'm from Texas and I've never heard of a 'car pool lane'."

"That's too bad. And besides that, you were not wearing your seat belt." I had neglected to reattach my safety belt after finding the map in the glove compartment.

Suddenly, I was going to get two traffic tickets when I had no idea I was doing anything wrong. It made me feel terrible. And, of all things, I was on my way to give my speech about hope and encouragement, and my audience was already there waiting for me.

I discovered that day that you cannot give away what you don't have. After listening to the police officer, I was so downhearted that I didn't have anything left to give. Worse, as I stood there while she wrote out the tickets, people in passing cars were honking and yelling at me out their windows, "Yeah, get him." "Get that criminal off the streets." I felt absolutely terrible.

It reminded me of the lesson on perception versus reality that I had learned when President Nixon visited Dallas. That time, people got the wrong idea about me because I was wearing ratty clothes and driving a beat-up car. This time, they thought I was a crazy hot-rodder. If I had been driving my usual four-door sedan, people would have had a different impression entirely.

As I stood on that busy highway, with the red lights on the police car flashing, I realized I would never make a good criminal. I would feel too bad about what others thought of me.

When I finally got back on the road toward the place where I was to speak, I was totally drained. It was clear that I needed self-encouragement, that I had to do something to get going again before I appeared before my audience. I didn't know what to do.

I reached the hotel, walked into the lobby, and looked around trying to think of something to perk me up. Then I saw a shoe-shine stand in the lobby and I thought that might help. It always makes me feel better to get a terrific shoeshine. So I jumped up on the stand and sat down. As I looked down at the shoeshine man, I saw one of the biggest smiles I've ever seen on anybody. Looking straight at me, he said, "Boy, it sure is good to have you here."

This was in December, right before Christmas, and he started talking about his wife and their new baby and how excited he was that this would be their first Christmas together as a family. He said that this was a part-time job to pick up some extra money for the holidays and for all the expenses of a new baby.

For a minute or two, I thought, "Boy, what a line to work up a good tip right before Christmas," but as he kept talking, I sensed his sincerity. He was excited and full of life, so much so that he was encouraging me. He was on top of the world, right there at the foot of a shoeshine stand.

I have always believed that one of the best ways to cheer your-self up is to encourage other people, so I understood quite well the effect he was having on me. Because I believe so strongly in encouraging others, I have a tradition that I call "My Monthly Tip." I always have a twenty-dollar bill handy that I give as a tip to someone who might never expect to get a tip of that size. I give it to someone who especially touches my life with kindness or encouragement — a dishwasher, a busboy, a porter, or a waiter in a place where there aren't usually large tips.

When he was through with my shoeshine, I was so filled with

happiness at being around a person like him that I gave this fellow my monthly twenty-dollar bill. He looked up at me and said, "I don't have change for a twenty yet."

"I don't want any change," I said and, at that, he got tears in his eyes. Then he started crying and I started crying and we hugged each other, and I walked away from that shoeshine stand feeling like a million dollars. Someone had touched me with encouragement and I had been able to do something nice for him.

Since I had been so rattled by the incident on the highway, I had already decided that I couldn't use my planned speech. I didn't know at first what I would say, but the experience with the shoeshine fellow gave me all I needed. I took the warm glow he had given me right into that room and gave one of the best speeches of my life, merely by telling them about what had happened to me that day.

If someone with a crystal ball had told me all about the cop on the highway before it happened, and given me the option to miss it, I would have accepted. If I had missed the cop on the highway, I would have walked right past the shoeshine stand and would never have had that important experience. If I had missed the cop and the shoeshine stand, that day would have been merely one more speech instead of standing out as a high point in my life.

### *WORKING IN THE "HUMP YARD"*

That wasn't the first time I'd found something positive in an incident that looked negative at the start. During the summer after my sophomore year in college, I had a job as a switchman with the Rock Island Railroad. Two events occurred that summer that I've always remembered as illustrations of how we can learn from emergencies.

One of the most memorable things that has ever happened to me was that my life was saved by a fellow worker one night in the rail yard. We worked together on the midnight shift and, since I was new, he was showing me the ropes.

When this incident happened, we were at a place you'll find in all rail yards that they call the "hump yard." The way they make up trains is to have a switch engine move around strings of cars and then push them over "the hump." The cars then roll down by gravity and slam together so they are automatically coupled, without the engine having to push them all together one by one. An individual in a control tower simply throws switches electrically as the cars roll down the hump, directing them to couple with the proper train.

As we were walking across the tracks in the middle of the night, I stepped across a hump and was immediately jerked backward off my feet by my shirt collar. A split second after my companion pulled me clear, a boxcar rolled silently by going about fifteen miles per hour. I had never imagined it was possible for a boxcar to approach with no discernible noise. However, without an engine nearby, that boxcar was gliding quietly along after crossing the hump, and it could not be heard above the ambient noise of the yard.

I never would have seen that car and surely would have been killed. Instead, because the Rock Island Railroad's policy was that new people had to be accompanied in the yard by someone with experience, I was with a man who knew the hazards and was watching out for me when I never expected danger.

## ACCURATE COMMUNICATION IS CRITICAL

The other memorable occurrence that summer taught me forever the importance of accuracy in communication. Because a railroad engineer could be as much as a mile away from trouble at the other end of the train, we had signals in the yard that helped the switchman to tell the engineer what was going on. During the day, communication wasn't much of a problem because you could see each other well enough even across the distances. Because I was a temporary summer employee, I only had the luxury of daylight hours while I was learning my job, and it wasn't long before I was off the day shift.

The first time I worked at night, communication became a

different story. We had to use flares to give signals to the engineer. The darkness did not seem to hamper communication much and the flares worked, until the first time I found myself at the end of a mile-long train.

Though the signalman was a mile away, I easily saw his flare. But then my eyes caught another signalman. And another. Suddenly, I could see that there were several people signaling with flares at the same time. I took a few seconds to make sure which one was for me and then flipped my switch to direct the oncoming car down the track that the signalman had instructed me to with his flare.

Soon after the car went by my position, I heard a great commotion around the corner from where I was. I raced toward the sound and discovered that the last car I switched had crashed into another train. While I believed I was doing the right thing, I actually had watched the wrong man, responded to the wrong signal, and sent a car down the wrong track.

The railroad didn't do anything to me for making that mistake because I had correctly followed the signal I saw. They realized that it was not an unreasonable mistake for someone new who was working for the first time at night to follow the wrong signalman. They now use radios in the yards to do what we did then with signal flares, but I learned that even the best advice given in the wrong context can be dangerous.

## THE ENERGY OF CHALLENGES

You can be sure that crises will occur, but you never know where they may lead. Given their certainty, your best response is to let their energy propel you to new horizons.

Ray Murray was a businessman in Florida who had sent about fifteen of his people to a seminar I taught. He had never attended one personally, but he had seen the results they produced in other people. Finally, Ray decided it was time to meet me, so he flew into San Antonio, where I was conducting a three-day seminar.

Ray and some of his people came out in the middle of the

summer, and you can imagine what San Antonio's days are like in July. I rented a big Lincoln to pick them up at the airport. When I got to the arrival pickup point, they were already waiting, so I pulled over, popped the latch on the trunk, and hopped out to help them load their luggage. Since it was so hot, I left the car running so the air conditioner would keep it cool inside.

After I got them all loaded up, I went around to open the door and found that it was locked. I couldn't understand how that had happened because I knew you couldn't lock the door from the outside unless you had the key. I certainly had not used the key, because it was inside in the ignition switch. Nonetheless, there we were, standing outside in the blazing afternoon Texas sun with every door locked tight.

One of the vice-presidents of Ray's company told me that this car model, which had a number keypad on the door, also had a new feature that automatically locked all the doors if you got out with the engine running. It's a great safety feature, because no thief will be able to jump in and drive away if you leave it running. However, the whole safety plan is dependent upon your knowing the keypad combination to get back inside.

Now the traffic was piling up behind us. There were the executives I was trying to impress, and I was looking across the car at them wondering if they were thinking I was a real Texas clod. It was terribly embarrassing that I had to leave them there and go inside to call the rental car company. Fortunately, I found the right person quickly, the combination was punched into the keypad, and we were soon on our way.

*Mistakes Can Open Doors*

This was not a good first impression to make on the president of a multi-million-dollar corporation who had come to see the motivational speaker for whose services he was spending so much money. However, the story had a happy ending because everyone had a sense of humor, and we all had a good laugh.

The seminar that weekend went well and Ray Murray and I became close friends. Since that first meeting, we have done a lot of business together, he has invited me down to cruise on his boat in the Bahamas, and I have flown his plane. Over the years, he has continued to send many people to attend my seminars and our friendship continues to grow. Had I not gotten us locked out of that Lincoln, my friendship with Ray would have never developed the same way.

A mistake can open you up, showing your vulnerability, illustrating how you handle a crisis, and creating an opening for friendship to enter. We all make mistakes, but many people are afraid to risk admitting them. This was a case where the first impression broke the ice and made me a real person to Ray. He already knew I was an impressive seminar leader; now he saw that I was real and could make mistakes. Allowing people to see your flaws along with your strengths can be the basis of a solid and lasting friendship.

### Beware of the Doomsayers

There is a danger when a crisis arises that people will listen to the doomsayers and think they're in a hopeless situation. Those are the times you need to remember that you are a self-encourager, press on through the crisis, and look for ways to come out the other side better than you were before it happened.

In November of 1857, *The Boston Globe* carried this startling headline: "Energy Crisis Looms — World to Go Dark." A subheading underneath said, "Whale Blubber Scarce." Can you imagine anyone today worrying about a shortage of whale blubber? Today, in fact, whaling is at an all-time low and we've got less whale blubber than ever. Nonetheless, in 1857, that problem seemed to augur the end of civilized life as it was then known.

Clearly, there have been times in every age when people believed the end was near and we would all freeze or starve to death. Yet, each of those challenges has always been met with improvements in technology.

During one of our more recent energy crises, in 1973, few experts would have believed you if you said that, in 1988, there would be a glut of oil on the market. There would have been further skepticism if you had said that the 1988 price of oil, corrected for inflation, would be lower than at any time since World War II.

### Relishing the Power of Crisis

Some people fully understand the power of crises and almost hope for them. I saw one example of this when I worked at IBM while the president was Thomas Watson, Jr.

At one time, when IBM was enjoying some astounding successes, Thomas Watson told some of his executives that they needed to double their failure rate. He knew that during great crises, great breakthroughs are made, and he felt that if they could experience the pressure of a crisis, it would help them maintain growth. He feared that continued success on the level they were then experiencing would set them up for a period of decline.

Another side to Thomas Watson's philosophy is that if people are not making many mistakes, if they never experience a crisis or an emergency, they are not pushing themselves hard enough toward growth. When the error rate is low, that can be a sign that individuals or companies are not doing much to stretch their limits. A painless way to do this, with minimal risk of failure, is to simulate mentally the changes you wish to make.

*Today's modern aircraft simulators are so realistic that a pilot can learn to fly a new aircraft type without ever being in the real plane. Simulator technology has progressed so far that the first landing a pilot makes in the actual airplane can be on a regularly scheduled commercial flight with passengers on board.*

# 10

# SIMULATOR TRAINING

Eastern Air Lines (may it rest in peace) introduced the Boeing 757 to the commercial airline industry, and was the first airline to have the new high-tech simulators for the 757. The story goes that an Eastern captain finished his training in the simulator and was certified by the FAA to operate the new jet.

If an airline has the latest-model simulators, current FAA regulations allow an experienced captain to check out solely on the ground. The captain's first time in the plane will be on a revenue trip with paying passengers on board, but the captain must be accompanied for his first twenty-five flight hours by a company check captain flying as his co-pilot. Still, his first landing ever in the new plane is on a regular trip with passengers.

A particular captain finished his training at Eastern's training center in Miami and went home to Atlanta to await his first assignment. He soon got a "short call-out" because there was a 757 already sitting at a gate in Atlanta with passengers on it, but no captain. Eastern had found a check captain, so they grabbed the newly checked-out captain for his first trip. He went to the airport, walked down the jetway, boarded the plane, and entered the cockpit. He shook hands with the check captain and they "pushed back," bound for Washington's National Airport.

The flight was routine, they landed safely, and the new captain stood in the doorway saying good-bye to passengers who had no idea they had witnessed his first landing in a 757. To the shock and horror of the senior flight attendant, when the last passenger deplaned, the captain asked her for a tour of the plane. He didn't know what the cabin looked like because he had never even *seen* a real Boeing 757 before. After his cabin tour, he went outside and walked around it on the ramp to admire the plane he was now qualified to fly.

## IT'S THE REAL THING!

Years later, I got to see the marvels of these new simulators firsthand. I was speaking at Delta Air Lines in Atlanta. When one of the vice-presidents heard that I once was an airline pilot myself, he invited me to fly their new Boeing 757 simulator. He let me sit in the captain's seat on the left, and he occupied the co-pilot's seat.

He took me through all the checklists, then turned to me and said, "Well, Patrick, where would you like to go?"

I said, "Let's go to Dallas."

He punched a few buttons and told me to take off. As we "rose into the air," the Dallas skyline appeared on the horizon. One of their simulator instructors served as an air traffic controller and gave me radar vectors to the airport landing pattern. Then I got to shoot an approach and landing to my home airport in a Boeing 757, without leaving this small room in Atlanta, Georgia. If I had been transported there blindfolded, I would have thought it was the real thing.

The true purpose of airline simulators is to train pilots to handle emergency procedures. It is generally thought in the airline business that pilots only earn their salaries when an emergency occurs, but then they earn every penny of it in a few seconds. The practice they get in the simulators is the key factor in whether a pilot can respond correctly to an emergency.

## WITNESS TO THE BIRTH OF A NEW WORLD

An Air Force pilot friend of mine got to see a demonstration of the visual simulators when they first came out. He had flown a group of highly experienced Air Force pilots out for a demonstration of the new simulator technology, to determine whether the Air Force needed them. The group, mostly generals, all piled into the cockpit of a simulator for the Air Force's then-new cargo plane, the giant C-5 Galaxy. Since it was so crowded in the simulator cockpit, all the VIPs had to remain standing. A test pilot occupied the left seat and had positioned the plane at the end of a runway for takeoff.

As the pilot shoved the four throttles forward, the sound was exactly as in the real aircraft, and everyone instinctively held onto something for balance against the feeling of acceleration. As the aircraft's speed increased, the runway raced past. Then, just before the plane attained flying speed, an alarm bell rang and one of the engine fire warning lights filled the cockpit with an ominous red flash. The pilot yanked all the throttles to idle and initiated what is considered to be the most dangerous maneuver a pilot can tackle in a jet transport — a high-speed abort.

Though the test pilot worked frantically to stop the speeding airplane, it was clear he wouldn't make it and a crash off the end of the runway was imminent. Everyone standing in the cockpit instantly grabbed anything they could to brace for the apparent crash. As the plane plowed off into the dirt, the pilot let go of the controls, stood up, and laughed. He turned around to see all those wide-eyed generals holding on for dear life while the "plane" careened across the airfield. The Air Force bought the new simulators.

## YOU CAN'T RISK LEARNING THE HARD WAY

Before simulators reached the highly developed state they are in today, a lot of emergency procedures had to be taught in actual aircraft. The danger in doing this was that the aircraft's performance was reduced, and accidents have occurred during practice emergencies.

Among the most dangerous maneuvers to practice in a real airplane was an engine failure during takeoff. The emergency was so hazardous, in fact, that the Air Force prohibited its pilots from practicing it. It wasn't a great situation that Air Force pilots never got to practice the most critical procedure they might ever encounter, but the Air Force felt that if it permitted engine failure maneuvers, a crash eventually would occur during training.

Scott Air Force Base near St. Louis, Missouri, is the home base for the Air Force's fleet of medical evacuation planes, known as the C-9 Nightingale. One day, many years ago, two pilots took an Air Force C-9 out on a training flight. One pilot was an instructor and the other was receiving recurrent training.

Right after takeoff, they encountered an actual engine failure accompanied by a fire warning bell. The pilot in training was flying and he immediately reached up and pulled one of the engine fire handles. The fire handle on a jet aircraft engine shuts off everything to that engine. That's an important safety feature to isolate the engine so that any fire will no longer be fed by fuel.

Unfortunately, because he had had no actual practice with this emergency, the pilot grabbed the fire handle for the wrong engine, cutting off everything on the good engine. They were barely off the ground and there was no time to get the good engine running again. In the investigation, they found that the last words on the cockpit voice recorder were "I'm sorry! I'm sorry!"

It is unlikely you will ever make a mistake that will take another person down with you as spectacularly as that poor pilot did. Nonetheless, you could simulate business scenarios and practice them mentally so you would be less likely to make mistakes that could ruin the financial security of your co-workers. Or you could

111

imagine various emergencies in your car and mentally practice how you would respond. Simulation might help you save a life or two after all.

## SIMULATE YOUR BUSINESS

As a business professional, you could simulate your next promotion, trying to imagine how it would look and feel. Visualize what changes you would find in your daily life. Would there be more phone calls? Would you meet different people? Would your hours, and therefore your commuting arrangements, be different? What adjustments would you have to make? Think all these things through during a quiet time, so that they will not be foreign to you when they happen for real.

Mentally move yourself into the new space and act as though you were there. What equipment would you need? What training might be helpful? What would you wear? You won't come up with all the answers, but you'll be better prepared than if you wait for a pressing situation to be at hand and then try to wing it.

Simulation is available to everyone all the time. You can start today; simply sit and quietly concentrate. Meditation can be a valuable tool.

Many people think that to be a success you must be able to think on your feet with a killer instinct. Others are in motion so much that few feel they can take the quiet time to simulate the future. Sitting at a desk and thinking does not have the outward appearance of accomplishing anything, and, truthfully, it does not accomplish anything tangible right then. People would rather do something — *anything* — that gives any sort of result *now!* Our continual focus on the bottom line for the next quarter often keeps us from taking a longer view. From the mailroom to the boardroom, you can benefit by simulating your next move.

One result of mental simulation is that it often shows you some things you can begin doing right away. Even if the list is not all-inclusive, it will be a starting point and you will be doing things you would not have thought of otherwise.

## *DOES VISUALIZATION ACTUALLY WORK?*

I'm sure you've noticed that I don't usually back up my anecdotes with studies and statistics. However, there is some clinical proof of the effectiveness of visualization.

Researchers at the University of Chicago conducted a study of visual simulation using three groups of students. The students' performance at shooting basketball free throws was measured separately for each of the three groups. Then, for the next thirty days, Group One did not take a single basketball free-throw shot. Group Two practiced foul shots on a basketball court every day for thirty minutes. Group Three practiced foul shots only in their minds for thirty minutes each day.

At the end of the thirty-day test period, the students came back to the court for a rematch. Group One showed no change in its shooting percentage, Group Two improved its shooting by 24 percent, and Group Three, the students who had only visualized shooting baskets, showed an astonishing improvement of 23 percent.

Some of the best nonclinical proof of the effectiveness of mental simulation can be found in the stories of our Vietnam prisoners of war. Some of them were in captivity for more than seven years, much of it spent in isolation. These men used their minds to simulate doing the things they used to do, such as golfing, playing the guitar, and playing the piano.

Some even learned to play instruments they had never played before, after other prisoners showed them the finger and hand movements. Then, without ever touching a real instrument, they assimilated the knowledge by mentally visualizing themselves playing the instrument.

My Air Force pilot friend, Ron, whom I've mentioned before, witnessed some of the powers that the Vietnam POWs developed during their captivity. Ron flew regularly with former POW Dave Luna, who became an accomplished chess player during his seven years in North Vietnam, and who learned to do it without a chessboard.

One day when they were flying together, Dave challenged Ron to a game of mental chess. Ron held his own for a while, but finally Dave said, "Bishop to queen's knight six, checkmate."

There was a brief discussion of the position of the pieces on their invisible board because Ron was certain that the bishop was blocked. Dave drew out the board for him, following the moves they had played and, sure enough, Ron's king was standing there wide open. With a real board, he never would have allowed that to happen. Unfortunately for Ron, Dave's practiced mental abilities didn't need a board to see the opening.

Simulators now allow airlines to practice for the most deadly situation in all of flying: wind shear. Simulator computers have been programmed using data taken from the sophisticated "black boxes" carried on airplanes that have crashed in wind shear conditions. This gives every pilot the chance to practice maneuvering an aircraft in conditions that have killed a lot of people.

## THE SUICIDE SQUAD — SIMULATION AT WORK

Simulation techniques have been used for decades by many organizations other than the airlines. You don't need sophisticated multi-million-dollar technical marvels for effective simulation. Sometimes all you need is a few dopey college freshmen.

As I was finishing my high school football career, I thought I had a good chance to continue playing in college. Naturally, living in Dallas, many people told me I should be a Longhorn and play for the University of Texas. While that had plenty of appeal, I also thought of looking around at other universities. With a name like "O'Dooley," where would you think I would be drawn? You guessed it: Notre Dame.

It was a hard decision for me because I liked both schools and, at the time, Texas and Notre Dame seemed to play each other regularly in the Cotton Bowl. It wasn't long before these two giant universities were fighting over me. Notre Dame wanted me to play at Texas and Texas wanted me to play at Notre Dame.

*I Was a Teenage Simulator*

I wound up at the University of Oklahoma, playing football for the Sooners. Back then, freshmen were not allowed to play on the varsity team; instead, there was a separate freshman team that served as a kind of simulator.

This freshman team had several wonderfully descriptive nicknames — The Suicide Squad, or Live Bait. Our mission was to emulate the playing style of whomever the varsity would play the following week, so that our team could practice against their coming opponent's game plan.

Oklahoma's game simulation was so real that each week they had us poor Live Bait guys wear jerseys with the names and numbers of the next opponent. Each Suicide Squad player's assignment was to learn the playing style and the route patterns of the opposing player whose number he wore all week.

*Paying Dues*

One of the biggest games in college football, and one of the longest-standing rivalries, is the annual Oklahoma-Texas game played in Dallas at the Cotton Bowl before a national television audience of 30 to 40 million viewers. In that region of the country, it's more of a major social event than a sporting event. It's always sold out and getting tickets to the game is a real status symbol. The city of Dallas is taken over that entire weekend by crazed fans who turn the pregame activities into a real circus.

My freshman year, the Texas game was played after one of our open weeks, which meant we did not play the week before the game. Therefore, we had two weeks to prepare for that year's game.

As the game neared, I was particularly glad to see the last day of our practice with pads. I had been assigned to play the position of a great Texas split end, wearing his jersey, name, and number for two weeks. Since he was one of the major keys to their offense, I became a special target, sort of a kamikaze pilot of the Suicide Squad. After two weeks of this special attention, I was beat up

*115*

pretty badly and looked forward to the actual game with more anticipation than most people.

I remember one Texas play I particularly hated that was called by our Suicide Squad quarterback, Bobby Warmack. I felt dread the instant I heard him call the play, because it called for me to throw myself as a blocker into our All-American linebacker, Carl McAdams. However, Bobby Warmack was great at getting us fired up. We went out on that field and he said, "All right, guys, go out there and give them a good lick, we've got to get 'em ready for Texas. It'll be on *one*. Ready! Break!"

I went out on the field and split way out wide. Bobby barked out the signals and on "Hut one," I jumped right across the line, in front of the person across from me, just as the play had been drawn. He released me because he thought I was going out for a pass.

As soon as he let go, I made my turn and headed on down the line, right at Carl McAdams. I was going full speed straight at him and he didn't see me coming. The thought instantly flashed through my brain, "I'm going to get a blindside hit on Carl McAdams."

I put my head down, smashed into Carl at full speed and knocked him end over end. It's one of those marvelous hits you dream about, the kind you might see in highlight films where everyone who sees it moans for the poor guy who got plastered.

When you got a good hit like that, it was football protocol that you pick yourself up and strut back to the huddle. Well, I was on my way back to the huddle, strutting my stuff and patting myself on the shoulders: "Patrick, that was a great hit. You just nailed Carl McAdams, an All-American linebacker! You done real good."

Suddenly, over my shoulder, I saw him coming at me, racing across the field. Not Carl McAdams, but one of our coaches, "Mad Dog" James, who was tagged with that moniker because when he got mad, he would yell and scream and literally foam at the mouth. He was running and screaming and looking like a wild man, already foaming at the mouth. I thought I was dead, but he raced right past me over to Carl, who was still lying on the ground.

*116*

The coach picked Carl up by his face mask, lifted him up in the air, and screamed, "What are you gonna do, McAdams? Are you gonna let some little freshman knock you on your can? What are you gonna do in front of 30 million people?" Then he turned to Bobby Warmack and screamed out, "Now run it again!"

The only thing about the next play that I remember was waking up when it was over.

*Taking Your Lumps When the Costs Are Low*

Sometimes in life we have to do things we don't want to do, but we do them anyway because they help get us where we want to go. My role in that game simulator had served to show Carl McAdams and the coaches what could have happened in the actual game. Imagine if it had been that Texas superstar split end who got the shot on Carl instead of a little freshman. Because the simulator had shown everyone a possibility they had not considered, Carl was prepared for the game.

The great part about all the punishment I took during those two weeks was that Carl did not get hit by that split end even once during the game. Though Texas ran the same play several times, Carl was always ready for it. As with a pilot in an aircraft simulator practicing a dangerous emergency, Carl was able to take his lumps when it didn't count. Pilots who crash in a simulator are usually embarrassed and have been known to need a break before resuming the simulator flight. Yet, as humiliating as a simulator crash is for an experienced pilot, it is obviously nothing compared to the real thing. A pilot usually relives a simulator crash over and over in his mind, and likely will never get in that situation in a real aircraft.

By simulating as many of your life experiences as you can, you can prepare yourself in ways you never would have imagined before the simulation. If the coaches had merely discussed that play with Carl in preparing for the Texas game, Carl probably would have thought there was no way he could be blindsided.

## PUT SIMULATION TO WORK IN YOUR LIFE

People who have wanted to change or reenter a career path have often used volunteer work to develop experience. If you look around, there is almost always some way to step into that next role and practice. It might be a class or a seminar, or something truly bold.

A fellow named Barry went to college, majored in fine arts, and wanted to be a TV cameraman. TV camera work is much more complicated than many people imagine. It's quite a skill to be able to look into a TV camera monitor and imagine what it will look like on the screen, taking into account shading, how the colors will change with the lighting, and movement.

When Barry got out of college he had no professional experience and found that no one would give him a job. Yet, he was determined to succeed; after all, he had filed his personal flight plan.

He was fortunate that his parents were supportive of his career goal and he was able to live with them for a while, which kept his living costs low. He volunteered to operate a camera at a local Public Broadcasting System station for no pay. With the tight budgets on which most PBS stations operate, they were glad to have him. He worked there for a solid year, acting as a regular employee, working a normal schedule and even taking overtime assignments. By the end of the year, he had a résumé, he had clips of his work, and he had shows that had been broadcast.

He then went out to Southern California to enter the movie industry. While it took some time knocking on doors in Hollywood, his work background gave him the credibility he needed to get hired. Of course, he started out at the lowest possible position, but there he was, working on movies in Hollywood when little more than a year earlier small television stations wouldn't even talk to him.

Barry has become well known enough to remain steadily employed in Hollywood, working on several motion pictures a year and earning a comfortable living. Without realizing it at the time, he had used my recommended simulator technique by putting himself in a giant TV cameraman simulator and training himself to handle the big job when it came to him.

If you are determined, you, too, can put yourself into such a simulation environment in almost any profession and prepare yourself for the real thing.

*Checkrides and recurrent training are routine for all airline pilots and occur at specified intervals: one year for co-pilots and flight engineers, and every six months for captains. Crew members are also subject to "no-notice" checks while flying regular trips with passengers; they never know when a company or FAA check-airman will show up for the flight and ride along in the cockpit jumpseat to observe their performance.*

# 11
# CHECKRIDES AND RECURRENT TRAINING

Few of us have checkrides in our lives, or anything like them. While there may be special occasions when you are called on to perform to your best standards, few people have another person watching their every move during a day on the job.

The pressure of a pending checkride helps a pilot to brush up on the basics and remain alert between checks for changes and improvements to procedures. To help stay sharp, you could build the equivalent of a pilot's checkride into your life.

The little things in life can have a major impact on our overall effectiveness. We are creatures of habit; we don't often break old habits, but instead form new ones. A checkride can be a time when the fallacy of an old habit can be revealed and we can replace it with something that is more effective.

Seek out people in your life in whom you have enough confidence that you can ask them to serve as checkpilots. In thinking about people who can fill this role, don't overlook the person you trust the most: yourself. Most of us have bad habits, things we would never do if a checkpilot were watching over our shoulder, because we would hear about it in the debriefing. When you next get the urge to do something you're glad nobody will see you do, imagine that your checkpilot is looking over your shoulder. Since you have more interest in the excellence of your performance than any outside observer, you will be your own toughest checkpilot.

If you have risen to a high position of power within your company, you probably have discovered that your actions are rarely challenged. Nearly everyone would like to eliminate being supervised, yet attaining that goal can cause a decline in our performance. It is probably ten times easier to allow your effectiveness to fall off when you know that no one will confront you about having a lackadaisical attitude.

Remember that even the most experienced, senior airline captain will go into a classroom twice a year for recurrent training or a checkride. When you get a chance to review your work with an observer, or you get a chance for some sort of refresher, please be open to all the help you can get. Your ego isn't on the line, but your attitude may be.

## *ARE YOU OPEN TO CRITIQUES?*

A few years ago, I met a group of people who don't have much interest in recurrent training. It happened when I spoke in Australia.

I always remember the flight over there. Way out in the middle of the ocean, the captain came on the speaker system and said, "Ladies and gentlemen . . . welcome to tomorrow." It seemed amazing to me that I had suddenly jumped ahead to another day. Since then, when I'm a little down, I'll call a friend in Australia and ask, "How are things tomorrow?" The Australians I know are such a positive group that I always can count on them to say that things are great. That way, I always know that tomorrow will be a good day, because it already is!

Once while I was in Australia giving a sales seminar and listing several important points, the audience kept yelling out, "B.T.D.T., B.T.D.T."

Finally, my curiosity aroused, I asked, "Okay, what does B.T.D.T. mean? Is that some sort of a disease or some curse you put on speakers?"

They said, "It means, 'Been there, done that.' " What they were telling me was that I wasn't saying anything new. They had already been there and done what I was saying, and they saw no point in hearing it again.

My belief is that you've never "been there and done that." No matter what you've done, even if you go back to the same spot and attempt to do the same thing, you will be doing it as the different person you have become. We are always changing as we go through life. We move on and we gather new experiences. You can go back, but you'll do things differently, with a different perspective.

Also remember the quotation I used in the Introduction, "Mankind has a far greater need to be reminded than informed." The importance of repetition in learning is one of the major points behind this book. Therefore, my philosophy is the opposite of the Aussie philosophy that was yelled at me from the audience. Over there, if they've heard something before, they don't ever want to hear it again. I've done some things many times and, no matter how many times I do them, each time is a unique challenge.

## THERE IS ALWAYS SOMETHING TO LEARN

Recording speeches for the Automotive Satellite Television Network (ASTN) is one of those unique challenges. The ASTN brings speakers to Dallas to feature on its satellite network. Automobile dealers subscribe to the channel so they can get the latest news and tips on the industry. The network offers discussion about the entire gamut of dealership issues, including information about customer service, maintenance service, advertising, etc. The schedule of shows is published in advance and the dealers often program their VCRs to tape the shows they want.

I remember the first time I was asked to speak on their network because they have a strict time constraint of *exactly* twenty-two and one-half minutes. I am accustomed to speaking to a live audience and getting their feedback, thinking on my feet and energizing myself from the reactions in the room. I knew that ASTN was going to be a checkride for my speaking talents.

When I got into the studio, I saw the camera, a few bright lights, a cameraman, and a digital clock. That was it. I had to fit my speech perfectly in to the next twenty-two and one-half minutes — and in addition get my message across. It was so different from anything I had done before. I would tell a joke, for instance, and the cameraman was the only one who laughed — only one person!

It felt like an audience of one, though in reality I had a captive audience of tens of thousands of people throughout the United States, Canada, and Mexico. When the cameraman laughed, I had to visualize that, somewhere, all those people were laughing also.

When I finished my message, I realized I had one minute and forty-five seconds to kill. So, I quickly thought of another point I could hit that tied in with what I had said earlier. Now the clock was ticking down: fifteen, fourteen . . . three, two, one. I had to wrap up my point exactly as the clock ran down, rather than according to what I might have wanted to say.

I had practiced my speech and had done it in exactly the right time, but it never goes the same way twice. So much for the "been there, done that" philosophy.

## QUALITY OF WORK LIFE

If you work for a large corporation, it will not be difficult to find check captains. American Airlines has an employee program called Quality of Work Life (QWL) that recognizes the importance of a high-quality work environment to its front-line, customer-contact people. I was fortunate to work with American Airlines, and the way it happened may seem accidental to some people, but I believe it was because I look for potential opportunities and I'm open to new ideas.

I was on my way home to Dallas on an American Airlines flight, and I had started a conversation with the lady sitting next to me. We were enjoying each other's company and making small talk.

I pointed out to the lady next to me the unmistakable enthusiasm of one of the flight attendants, noting my opinion that having employees like this was why American had grown so rapidly. My seatmate listened attentively as I raved about how great American Airlines' employees were, and how they contributed to the company's success.

Then my seatmate said, "Let me tell you about that lady." It turned out that I had been talking to American Airlines' West Coast flight attendant supervisor. "You won't believe this flight attendant's story," she continued.

"She has just returned to work after having a bout with cancer. And, as if that isn't enough, she has a felony charge pending against her because, during her illness, her husband left her, tried to take their child with him and, in a heated moment, she shot him in an attempt to stop him from taking her daughter."

She paused to let me pick up my dropped jaw, then continued: "On top of that, she is going to have to declare bankruptcy because of all the financial strain she's suffered during her troubles."

Watching the flight attendant on the job, I never would have known she had a care in the world. It was amazing to see that someone could appear that happy and enthusiastic while having so many troubles in her personal life. I told my seatmate about my line of work — encouraging people to do their best. She told me that my work sounded like something American Airlines could benefit from, and she referred me to another staff person at American, Susan Schiegel.

## A Personal Checkride

Susie, who was in charge of all the reservation managers around the country, asked if one of her staff, Maureen Burke, could come to hear me speak. I had a Dallas speaking engagement set up in November of 1987. I told Susie that Maureen was welcome to come, but that I was scheduled to speak at seven o'clock in the morning.

On the morning of my speech, I discovered that the company had taken my audience out on the town the night before. They had all been out very late and no one was in the mood to hear a speech, especially at 7:00 A.M. Not only were they tired, sleepy, and hung over, but the room was cold and dark. It all added up to a truly miserable atmosphere.

It was one of the toughest audience environments I have ever faced. It was to be a checkride for me with American Airlines and, if I passed, I might land a large deal. I am always optimistic, but on this day I was glad that I had some long experience with self-encouragement.

I noticed that Maureen Burke listened to my speech from the back of the room. When I was through, she left and I didn't have a chance to thank her for coming to hear me, especially so early in the morning.

The combination of the terrible setting, the early hour, and Maureen's rapid departure made me think that I had blown my opportunity to work with American Airlines. The audience had not been "with me" throughout my speech, and I never really won them over. I figured I had "flunked" my checkride.

As it turned out, Maureen liked what she had heard, she gave a favorable report to her boss, Susie Schiegel, and they hired me to speak at an American Airlines conference for reservation managers. At about the same time, another American manager, Ralph Richardi, told me that he had heard me speak and that he liked what he heard. It turned out that Ralph had started the QWL program at American, along with Bob Crandall, American's president.

Ralph was based in Los Angeles, in the West Coast Reservations

Office, and his main job at American was to encourage the employees to enjoy their jobs. Ralph invited me to come out and meet with him, so I flew to Los Angeles and interviewed before a panel of twenty American QWL managers to explain why I would be a good speaker for their QWL conferences.

One of the questions they asked me was how long it would take me to prepare a speech for a QWL conference. "I've been preparing for twenty years," I said. "I could give it tomorrow." They hired me and I spoke at one of their conferences.

*Needing Self-Encouragement*

After I did the QWL conference, American hired me for a special program. This involved speaking to their new hires during their orientation to the company about encouraging themselves while they're on the job.

Many airline employees, especially those at smaller airports, work alone. They rarely ever see a supervisor and, in fact, many supervisors would recognize only a handful of the workers for whom they are responsible because most perform their work hundreds or thousands of miles away.

Those airline employees who work alone are often the only contact that consumers have with the company. They may have to face an irate customer solo and, with no other employees to turn to for encouragement, simply move on to the next customer and treat them as nicely as possible. For most airline employees, self-encouragement is crucial: they've got to feel good about themselves and what they're doing.

*A "Positive" Checkride System*

American Airlines has a great program to help encourage their isolated workers. Their program is called AAdvantage Gold.

I fly American so often that I am a member of their AAdvantage Gold frequent-flier program, which means that I'm in the top 2 percent of the flying public on American Airlines. Through that program, the airline gives me a quarterly allotment of four special certificates that I can hand out to honor any of its employees who catch my attention for doing an extra-good job. The certificates I get to hand out say, "You are special!" and the employee can turn them in to the company for credit toward bonuses.

There are not many of these coupons around. Any employee who gets more than one a year is doing very well. Getting several a year indicates truly top-notch performance. All American employees know that any customer they meet could give them a certificate in recognition of their performance, because the employees don't know who the AAdvantage Gold customers are.

I like this program because it's a good chance to give a reward to people who are especially helpful. There is usually no easy way to thank employees of large corporations for that extra effort that may have made your day. With American, I get the chance to return some of the favors that the employees do for me.

Another good aspect of the AAdvantage Gold program is that it gives employees a chance to be called into a supervisor's office for good news. In most large companies, especially airlines, a summons to the supervisor's office is almost always bad news. This situation is remedied by American's attention to encouraging their employees and creating a positive work environment.

## MY BEST ELEVEN MINUTES

I once gave a speech at the Federal Land Bank in Chickasha, Oklahoma. Because Chickasha's airport didn't have lights, which would have prevented my leaving after my presentation, I flew my plane to a nearby town and drove to Chickasha.

This engagement was an after-dinner speech, which usually lasts thirty-five to forty minutes because after-dinner people want to be entertained a little and then sent on their way. Before booking the date, the meeting planner asked what I charge. I answered, then added that my fee was good for anything up to an hour. He said that if that's what I charged for an hour, he wanted an hour. I said, "Yes, sir, you're paying for an hour and if you want an hour, I'll be happy to give you the full hour."

When I arrived for the speech, I noticed that their printed program showed that the evening would be over precisely at ten o'clock. However, they gave out lots of awards and honored some of the old town fathers. They let each award winner speak and I kept watching the time as it drifted closer and closer to ten o'clock. Finally, the meeting planner leaned over to me and said, "How about giving me your best eleven minutes?"

I went through my one-hour speech like a computer doing a data search and picked out the best stories I had. I decided that instead of trying to talk fast and give them as many anecdotes as I could, it would be better to pick out the best point or two and offer those. I picked out what I thought were three key words and built a short presentation around them.

When I spoke, I didn't say one word about how long my planned speech was. I delivered the eleven minutes as if that was how it had been planned, with no apology for how an hour's speech might have been. That was one of my toughest checkrides, but, because of the simulation and training I had put myself through, I was ready; I gave them my best eleven minutes.

Even though you have to prepare fully for every checkride, you have to be flexible. You can't be locked into any one way of doing anything. You have to be able to adjust. Instead of getting upset that they were being unreasonable, I saw it this way: they deserved the best I had. They only had time for eleven minutes, and they were going to get the finest eleven minutes I could give them.

Usually, when people are in a situation that turns out differently than they thought it would, they make things even worse by focusing on what "could have been." Instead of getting caught up in feeling cheated and wishing it could be done another way, strive to give your best. The people around you deserve it, and it will make you feel terrific.

Checkrides are not always done in fair weather. Pilots hate to take checkrides when the weather is miserable, but real professionals won't spend time worrying that their best would have been better under different conditions.

Sometimes, we simply lack the physical ability to reach our destinations. For a pilot's license to be valid, it must be accompanied by a current medical certificate, and some pilots have medical restrictions that will prohibit them from becoming airline captains. However, these restricted pilots may fly privately and as far as they wish, and some have flown well past where you might have expected them to go.

*A pilot's license is not valid without a current aviation medical certificate. The FAA qualifies pilots medically into one of three types of medical classes: first class, second class and third class.*

# 12
## MEDICAL CERTIFICATES

The third class medical certificate is the least restrictive; a person merely needs to be in generally good health to qualify for one. It is a prerequisite for becoming a student pilot and is as high as any pilot needs to fly privately. Third class medical certificates are good for two years.

To fly commercially, a pilot must pass a more rigorous physical examination to qualify for a second class medical, which is good for one year. After one year, it automatically reverts to a third class medical.

To qualify as a pilot of airline transport planes, an individual must pass a first class medical examination. The first class certificate is the most restrictive and requires the most rigorous physical examination of any of the medical certificates. It is valid only for six months; after that, it reverts to a second class medical for six months, then drops to a third class medical.

Not everyone can pass a first class medical. Some people have medical limitations that will always hold them back from attaining top-level performance in some areas. How much should a medical limitation hold us back from doing what we most want to do? It depends on a person's attitude.

Yes, attitude. Aptitude is a second-level factor that can easily be overcome with a strong and positive attitude. Through my professional speaking, I have learned a lot about the important influence of attitude on performance. One of the things I do during my speeches is to ask the audience to tell me what words they use to describe a winner.

I go to a board or a flip chart and as people in the audience call out the words they associate with winners, I write down the first ten I hear. Over the years, I have kept the lists people have given me and I have turned them into my Top Ten List of Winning Qualities.

## *THE TOP TEN WINNING QUALITIES*

Ranked in order of occurrence, from lists suggested by more than a thousand audiences, here are the ten qualities most associated with winners:

| | |
|---|---|
| 1. Positive attitude | 6. Optimistic |
| 2. Enthusiastic | 7. Dedicated |
| 3. Determined | 8. Happy |
| 4. Motivated | 9. Good listener |
| 5. Confident | 10. Patient |

It is significant to note the qualities that did not show up in the top ten. For example, none of the top winning qualities has anything to do with physical or mental ability.

Of course, you don't have to rely on my nonclinical study, because the famed Carnegie Institute conducted a study similar to mine that produced the following conclusion on what makes a person a winner: a winning formula is 15 percent aptitude and 85 percent attitude.

That's wonderful news for every human being alive. The lesson from both of these studies is that ANYONE can be a winner, because winning is based on attitude and not aptitude. Regardless of your natural abilities, *you* can control whether or not you will be a winner in life.

## *IF I CAN SUCCEED, YOU CAN SUCCEED*

When I conduct this informal survey in my seminars and I write down the list of winning qualities that people call out, invariably I will misspell at least one of the words. When I am done, I ask the audience if anyone sees anything wrong with what I wrote, and there is always someone in the crowd who has noted my spelling errors. To emphasize even further why a winning formula is based more on attitude than aptitude, I use my misspellings as a bridge to talk about my school days.

During my early school years, there were many teachers who thought I was a bit slow because I had a lot of trouble in school. It was not until junior high school that I was diagnosed as dyslexic. Though I actually have a high IQ, when I look at letters or numbers, my eyes sometimes reverse them in passing them to my brain.

While my teachers thought I didn't have a high aptitude, I've developed the one thing I do have total control over — my attitude. Throughout my professional years, my positive attitude has gotten me much farther than if I had had all the intellectual aptitude in the world.

## *IT DEPENDS ON HOW YOU USE WHAT YOU'VE GOT*

Another way of looking at your ability to be a winner is to say that it depends on what you do with the raw materials that you've got. Nearly any raw material can be made highly valuable with the right refinements.

For example, imagine that you are a five-pound bar of iron ore in its raw form. Also imagine that you know that some people are five-pound bars of gold ore. You are only worth about $5, but they begin life worth about $30,000. Imagine that neither of you will go any farther in life. If that is true, you will never amount to anything against the person who is made out of gold.

On the other hand, what would happen if you decided to work on your attitude and make your iron ore into something valuable?

Properly refined, you could become worth hundreds of thousands of dollars if you were made into watch springs, for example. You can go from a value of only $5 to a worth of hundreds of thousands of dollars if you use your energy to make the best possible use of what you have.

If you do this in life, you will pass millions of gold bars who are sitting around smugly admiring the value of their natural state. The truth is that few people put much work into refining their raw materials. You can never change the raw materials themselves, but the process of refinement is the one thing you can control.

*Against All Odds*

The great basketball star "Pistol Pete" Maravich was born with a congenital heart problem that kills most people by the age of eighteen. Yet, because of his dedication to physical conditioning, he lived to be forty and enjoyed a very successful career as a professional basketball player. He could have decided early in life that he wasn't made out of a precious natural resource. Instead, he refined what he had to the highest degree possible for him.

He died years after his professional career had ended, during a pickup basketball game. People asked, "How could this tremendous athlete, in such good health, kick off like that, so young?" The answer is that he didn't kick off at an early age; he lived more than twenty years beyond his life expectancy.

Have you ever known anybody who wasted the perfect health with which they were born? Of course, it happens all the time. Many men who were blessed with perfect bodies became complacent and succumbed to heart attacks at ages younger than Maravich, who suffered from a congenital heart problem.

Don't ever forget, it's 85 percent attitude.

*The Dream of Flight*

When I was growing up in Dallas, my father used to take us to Love Field to watch the airplanes take off and land. Back then, there was only one main runway at Love, and a dirt road only about fifty feet away from it was always crowded with hundreds of people watching the airplanes.

*133*

Those planes, coming and going from such exotic places as Waco, Big Spring, and Tulsa, were enough to get me hooked on the idea of becoming an airline pilot. My dad was a great encourager, and he told me, "Patrick, whatever you want to do, you can do it, but *you* have got to make it happen." I learned that lesson well at an early age.

You can't wait for someone else to take you where you want to be or make you feel better. What if that "someone else" never shows up? I decided to make myself into an airline pilot.

I worked hard through school, I went into ROTC in college, and then I flew all over the world in the military. When my tour was completed, I had all the qualifications I needed to become an airline pilot. However, when I separated from the military in the early 1970s, the country was in the middle of a recession and the airlines were not hiring pilots. In fact, the airlines were laying pilots off.

I knew the recession wouldn't last forever, so I decided to work at other jobs and maintain my flying skills by flying part-time until the airlines were hiring again. I went to work full-time for IBM, but at night, I put on my leather flying jacket and was transformed into "Patrick O'Dooley, Super-Pilot!"

I flew checks and mail all over the country, sometimes until two or three in the morning, and then I got up at six and went to work at IBM. I didn't care about the crazy hours because I was progressing toward my goal of becoming an airline pilot.

I discovered then how much more you can do than you might have expected when you are headed toward a destination instead of merely drifting along. All the years of work finally paid off one day when I was hired by Braniff Airlines. Although I was hired into the training department, I was in heaven because I could progress into a regular cockpit flying job. Soon I would be an airline pilot, and I was about as excited as anyone could possibly be.

Shortly after going to work at Braniff, I was home on a holiday break. I remember it well, because it was Christmas Eve and my first child, Timothy Kelly O'Dooley, was three years old. More than anything else, what Kelly wanted for Christmas was a fort in the backyard. We were outside working as hard as we could to get the fort done before dark. About four in the afternoon, I could see that we needed to work much faster, so I began pounding in those nails as fast and as hard as I could.

Then it happened. I hit one nail slightly off center and it came right back and struck me in the eye.

*From Gold Bar to Iron Ore — Instantly*

My wife took me to the hospital, but even with emergency surgery, I lost the eye. Along with the eye went my goal and my dream. In one split second, everything I had dreamed about was gone. I don't mind saying that I spiraled right down and hit rock bottom. I'd like to say that I hit rock bottom and bounced back up, but I didn't. I hit bottom, and I stayed there.

I couldn't see the point in going on. Nothing made sense to me anymore. I couldn't pull myself up. I had done so many things in my life that depended upon my physical ability that I equated that physical ability with myself.

After being down for months and feeling sorry for myself, I finally decided that I didn't like how I felt. I remembered what my dad had said earlier, "You can do whatever you want, but you've got to make it happen." I decided that what I wanted most was to stop feeling sorry for myself and enjoy life again.

I pulled myself up out of the muck and mire of self-pity and went to work developing another career. Today I am a successful professional speaker; but I never would have done it if I had not read all those books when I was recovering emotionally from the trauma of losing my eye.

Up to that point in my life I had perceived myself physically as a bar of gold. When I was changed instantly into iron ore, I learned how to refine what I was and become a winner.

I have to admit that I didn't do it entirely on my own. I have always encouraged people to be open to coaching from others, because you never know where you will find the piece to the puzzle that you need most. I had help in recovering from my self-pity over the loss of my eye, and it came from my three-year-old son, Kelly.

## TIMOTHY KELLY O'DOOLEY

Kelly was born in Germany while I was in the service. Even though he was born to American parents on an American military facility, Kelly got the rights of dual citizenship. So, technically, Kelly could live in Germany with all the rights of a full citizen.

Kelly came into the world in the same hospital room that General George S. Patton died in right after World War II. The room had been decorated as a memorial to General Patton and had photos of him and several plaques hanging on the walls.

One of the plaques contained a favorite quotation of the general's, "Success is not what you do when you're on top. Success is how high you bounce when you hit bottom." I always remembered that quote; it was very important to me after I lost my eye, and during the years I was developing my concept of self-encouragement.

Even the most successful people cannot be on top always, and self-encouragers realize that they're going to hit bottom at one time or another. When the inevitable bottoming-out happens, we've got to learn how to bounce.

When new parents describe the birth of their child, they often say that one of the first things they did was count all the fingers and toes. When Kelly was born, it was the most joyous moment of our lives but, while checking his fingers and toes, we discovered that his thumbs were not fully developed and were barely hanging on. The doctors removed one of them almost immediately.

Because of the surgery and the fact that he was born prematurely, we had to leave him in the hospital for two weeks after my wife was released. During that time, my wife, Beverly, and I kept a constant vigil over his progress. He was so tiny that I can remember being completely ecstatic when we heard that he had gained an ounce in a day.

As he got stronger, we saw that everything else about Kelly was fine. Since his health was perfect except for his missing thumbs, we counted our blessings for all the good that he possessed.

My military tour was nearing its end when Kelly was born, so we were faced with the question of where we would live after I got out of the service. One important factor in choosing a place to settle is where we would get excellent treatment for Kelly's hands. At that time, there were only three surgeons who specialized in hands, and one of them happened to be in Dallas. That fact, combined with others, helped us make the decision to settle there.

While we knew that Kelly was going to face a long series of operations to fix his hands, we were surprised when the doctor wanted to perform the first major surgery when Kelly was only six months old. The surgery was not a sure thing, so we faced a serious choice about Kelly's future.

The surgery the doctor had planned was to split Kelly's index fingers and move them off to the side into the place where a thumb would normally be. He would only have three fingers on his hand, but at least he would have that important opposing force that is the key to human manual dexterity. The biggest factor we had to consider was that the surgery had only about a 50-50 chance of success and, if it failed, Kelly might also lose his index fingers.

The doctor convinced us of the significance of the grasping power that Kelly would gain with the addition of thumbs. We came to see that there would be little difference between having three fingers or four fingers without any opposing digit to grasp against.

That surgery, when he was six months old, was the first in a series. There was one major operation every year for the first eight years of his life. Each time, they would build the thumbs a little more, taking ligaments and tendons from other parts of his body and implanting them in his hands to construct the parts he needed.

We felt sorry for this adorable little boy who had such troubles at such an early age, but Kelly was always a happy and positive child. He went through so much that he grew in his own way, developing other talents that he had the capabilities for. Despite his limiting condition, it was amazing to see how he would pick activities in which he could excel.

Kelly was in for a disappointment, however, because he wanted to play football like his father. He was never a large boy and, besides being too small for football, we couldn't let him play because of the sensitive condition of his hands.

Kelly's athletic prowess was not to be stopped by a little limitation like his hands, so Kelly discovered soccer. Once he started playing soccer, he grew to be among the best players on his team. His athletic prowess has extended to skiing, baseball, basketball, and golf, even though he only has 20 to 25 percent of normal strength in his thumbs. Kelly was never daunted by his troubles and, now almost grown, his hands do not hinder his activities at all.

Though we all face difficulties in our lives, if you focus on the positive aspects of your life instead, you can be happy despite your troubles. That's what self-encouragers do, and Kelly had a lot to do with helping me understand this important idea.

### NEAL JEFFRIES

I saw another example of attitude over aptitude in my friend Neal Jeffries. Neal was a great high school athlete out of Kansas, who went to Baylor University on a football scholarship and became its starting quarterback. Neal is now the youth minister at my church, and has become a close friend of mine.

Neal Jeffries stutters terribly. Can you imagine being the quarterback on a major college football team with a stutter so bad that sometimes you couldn't even start to talk? However, Neal had more determination than most people, and he has always found ways to work around his limitation.

When Neal had to call the plays, he had a hard time getting

started, though once he began to speak he was all right. Because of his difficulty in getting started, his teammates would help. In the huddle, the fullback would call the plays. When Neal came up to the line, if the other players could tell he was having a hard time starting the count, someone would call out something like "Blue!" That would be all Neal needed to jump-start himself into doing the count on his own.

With the help of his buddies, Neal overcame his stuttering and led his team to the championship of the Southwest Conference. That year, Neal Jeffries became the conference offensive player of the year. Neal has never used his stutter as an excuse for failure. He has always done things you would not expect from someone who stutters so badly.

Today, Neal speaks to youth groups all over the country and in front of our entire church congregation to give announcements. When speaking in public to people who don't know him, he always puts them at ease by beginning with, "As you will hear, I am a stutterer, but it's something I have overcome." Neal is great proof that the top ten qualities of a winner are all based on attitude.

Even if you are never limited by missing thumbs, losing an eye, or a terrible stutter, you can be sure that if you live long enough, you will eventually experience one kind of limitation or another. It's part of the human condition and, since it is, perhaps you ought to think about upgrading your rating.

*Jet aircraft can only be flown by pilots who hold a special type rating on their license for that particular plane. A rating for one large aircraft is not certification to fly another. Pilots who have flown the Boeing 747 for years and who switch to a 727 must have a type rating for the 727. Each rating requires an intensive ground school and flight training program.*

# 13
## TYPE RATINGS

In many fields of endeavor, a general educational background is insufficient to qualify an individual for specialized work. For example, simply because you have a degree in accounting doesn't qualify you to work in banking when your years of experience are in the oil and gas industry. Life today is too complex for one person to do everything, just as today's aircraft are too complex to allow one pilot to fly any jet he chooses.

In aviation, a 727 pilot most likely could get into any jet airliner, take off and land safely at another airport. Other than the landing, which might not be as smooth as one made by a pilot more experienced in that particular plane, the passengers might never know that the pilot was not rated for that aircraft. However, what if something unusual came up? If the weather at the arrival airport turned sour and the pilot had to land in low visibility or a strong crosswind, his inexperience in the new plane could prove fatal.

The principle of being rated for your own special niche applies to countless other areas in life. Consider the accountant with experience in the oil and gas field. If that accountant took on a client in another field, the client might never know the difference; or the accountant might overlook an unusually quirky circumstance that a specialized accountant would recognize without a second thought. The result could be financial disaster.

Today, more than ever, there are so many regulations and specialized paperwork in virtually every field that it may be irresponsible not to restrict yourself to expertise in one well-defined niche. The complexities in accounting have resulted in a requirement that accountants take a certain number of continuing education credits each year to maintain their certification. Therefore, in some fields, there already is a type-rating system of sorts in place.

*CALL A SPECIALIST*

I know a man who earned the designation of certified management consultant, which, theoretically, would qualify him to handle many of his own affairs. He might expect to be able to deal with his own real estate transactions, insurance, taxes, estate planning, and trusts for the kids. On the other hand, considering that the nature of our society is so complex, should this man pay for outside consultants? Yes, he should.

Most of us are reluctant to call a specialist. We may think it costs too much, it gives up control, it takes too much time to go to someone's office for a consultation — or, finally, our ego gets in the way. People think, "I'm as smart as he is, if he can do it, I can do it!" Actually, it has nothing to do with how naturally smart we are, and everything to do with the fact that we cannot be experts at everything.

Certainly, the captain of a 747 can learn to fly the smaller 727, and the 747 pilot may even have been rated in a 727 at one time. However, some of the safeguards and backups that are taken for granted in the 747 do not exist in the 727. A professional pilot knows that the current captain with a more recent 727 rating is better qualified.

A corollary in the business world might be an executive who worked for years in giant corporations and who decided to try his hand at running a smaller company. It would be erroneous for the executive to assume that he could duplicate his experience in large corporations in running the smaller company. For example, the executive may have taken for granted certain financial margins of safety in the fast-paced world of the major corporation, and these may not exist in a smaller company.

There is a world of difference in the experience and skill necessary to run a family-owned corporation, a limited partnership, a sole proprietorship, or part of a major corporation. Each kind of entity has its own quirks and nuances. Similarly, in flying, there are ratings for different types of aircraft such as seaplanes, gliders, hang gliders, and hot-air balloons.

## *UPGRADE BEFORE YOU* NEED *TO*

The various levels of ratings for pilots have corollaries in most aspects of life. The higher the rating, the better your chance of getting hired when you want to move on.

The time to upgrade your rating is when you are on autopilot, cruising through calm weather with the time to anticipate future needs. Perhaps you might consider that, though your last flight was in good weather, winter is surely coming. Will your current skills serve you if you get stuck in rotten weather next winter?

Too often, people upgrade their skills only when circumstances demand it. A private pilot who had been planning to get an instrument rating would find that his intentions to do so would not help him one whit if he was suddenly trapped above a thick layer of clouds.

If you elect to update your rating in life when you don't have to, but because you recognize its potential benefits, you will be much better served. First, you will not have to study for the upgrade while under other kinds of pressure. Second, knowing you can handle more complicated flying, you will increase your self-confidence in your current position. Think of yourself as a private pilot with an instrument rating who better enjoys the sightseeing on a clear day knowing that if the weather did sour, a safe descent through the clouds could be made on instruments.

Once your skills were upgraded, you would be ready if the situation on your job suddenly called for someone with higher qualifications. Furthermore, your superiors would be impressed not only that you had increased your skill level, but also that you are a person with enough vision to see that one day you would need them.

I put these principles to work in my own world of flying when I decided I wanted to fly an ultra-light aircraft. At the time, I had logged more than one thousand flight hours in larger and more complex aircraft. Yet, before I moved "down" to an ultra-light, I wanted to be sure I understood its special characteristics.

## *ADD NEW RATINGS*

I have described an ultra-light as a kite with a motor. You might imagine the original Wright Flyer, but made out of modern materials. The thrill of flying an ultra-light is that the pilot is out in the open with the "wind in his hair."

I had been fascinated by ultra-light aircraft for a long time. However, they're considered dangerous, and always before I flew a new plane, I went up first with an instructor who helped me get familiar with it. I tried to get instruction in flying an ultra-light, since they handle quite differently from normal airplanes, but that was not possible because they are all single-seaters.

Finally, an ultra-light model was produced that was big enough to have two seats, and I arranged for a training course. My instruction began with an intensive ground school, after which I was taken out to an ultra-light and shown all its features. With all this preparation, I felt confident that, at last, I could go up in an ultra-light safely.

I had dreamed about how great it would feel to be out in the open with the wind in my face, being close to nature as I flew through the air with more freedom than I had ever felt in a plane. Instead of feeling joy, however, all I felt was extraordinary discomfort.

I was mentally kicking myself for not relishing this fantastic experience. Nevertheless, despite all the training and more than a thousand hours of previous flight time, I was scared of this completely foreign environment.

The instructor didn't know how I felt and continued the lesson as planned. He first showed me how to do each maneuver and then let me practice. Soon I had a pretty good feel for how an ultra-light flew.

Then the instructor shut off the engine to show me how well it glided. It was clear that even if I lost all power in this machine, I could easily glide down and land nearly anywhere.

Once I got the feel of operating it like a glider, the instructor restarted the engine, which is about the same size as a lawn mower, by pulling on a rope. We returned to the airport and, after a few practice landings, we did a full-stop landing and I was officially checked out in an ultra-light aircraft.

Flying an ultra-light was even better than flying a real airplane. When I was aloft, out in the open like that, surrounded by nature instead of aluminum, I felt like an angel. It was so wild and free, I could even smell the fragrance of the fresh-cut alfalfa coming up from the fields below. It was a truly euphoric feeling.

After my initial checkout, I used to go out quite often to enjoy this new thrill. One time, I got into the aircraft and found that its engine was a little hard to get started. I got it started eventually and took off, but on the climb out I could sense that the engine did not have its usual power, and it continued to feel slow even after I was up to a good altitude. It wasn't unsafe, but it took a little more attention to keep it flying.

Toward the end of the flight, I was sightseeing at a low altitude, barely above the trees. I noticed a little knoll ahead that I would have to climb up to clear. Instinctively, I added a little power so the ultra-light would begin to take me over the trees that were on the top of the knoll. Unfortunately, I was so high on euphoria that I started too late to give it power and the engine sputtered. Seconds later, I crashed into the treetops on the knoll.

I realized later that this incident occurred as all aircraft crashes do: it was a series of small mistakes that accumulated into an accident. If the plane's engine had been working properly, or if I had not been caught up in the moment and timed the power differently when I saw the knoll, there would have been no crash. I'll never forget the embarrassment of having to walk back to the airport and tell the owner that I had crashed his ultra-light.

Things could have been worse. I was unhurt and the only damage to the ultra-light was a broken propeller, which I replaced. But I never forgot that day and, for years, I had the broken propeller hanging on the wall of my office with a sign underneath it that read, "Plan Ahead."

When the need to pour on the power becomes obvious, it is often too late. No matter where you are now, you are always going to be somewhere else soon because life never lets us sit in one place. It's great to look at the beauty and even enjoy a little euphoria as you cruise through life, but don't let it get in the way of planning ahead. Have you prepared what you will need when you arrive?

## NO DESTINATION IS EVER "ENOUGH"

Some people stay landlocked, never upgrade their "type ratings" in life because they believe they've already got all they need. As self-encouragers, we should be looking to the future and planning ahead no matter how great things look today.

One thing that has always driven me crazy is the attitude of some people who feel they are "born into" a certain level of life, and therefore don't need any "type ratings." I've seen this on both ends of the spectrum: people born rich who thought they were a superior form of life and people who believe they can never escape the shackles of growing up in a deprived environment.

I was at a speaking engagement in Galveston, Texas, and as I was greeting some of the dignitaries, I noticed that some of their name tags had the letters "BOI." After a while my curiosity got me and I asked what those letters meant. I was told they stood for "Born On Island."

Galveston is an island in the Gulf of Mexico off the Texas coast. To the people who live in Galveston, having been born on the island carries a lot of prestige. Even if you were born across the ship channel, your family moved onto Galveston when you were a baby, and you lived there the rest of your life, that's not at all the same as being "BOI."

I thought it silly to place so much value on the location of someone's birth. To do so seemed to discount an individual's talents and characteristics. Someone could be outstanding in every way, yet not get full recognition because the "BOI" label carries such importance. It seemed a shallow way to judge people.

There are plenty of talented people in Galveston, including engineers and scientists who work at the Johnson Space Center, and doctors who work at a large burn facility there. Nonetheless, to some on the island, no life accomplishment will ever compare with the esteem of the simple tag: "BOI."

Where you come from has nothing to do with where you can end up. High-tech planes can fly anywhere in the world, and so can you. You don't have to remain stuck in a terrible environment just because you were raised in one, and if you have flown into bad weather, there are lots of ways to get help. Just as the pilot can get help, you, too, can find a way to fly clear on top.

No one has to wish for a BOI name tag or be held back by the circumstances of birth. Community colleges offer courses at all hours on cable TV. With a programmable VCR anybody can learn nearly anything regardless of their work schedule. It's a matter of desire. Today in America, more than ever in our history and more than anywhere else in the world, your talent and determination are what get you where you want to go.

### YOU'RE NEVER TOO OLD TO LEARN

Is there a time in life when you should stop learning and settle down to "be" whatever you are? I think not. I recently heard of a woman who entered college at the age of sixty-eight and had earned three master's degrees by the time she was seventy-nine.

Then she started working on her doctorate. Her decision to be a college student was fully supported by her ninety-seven-year-old mother.

I knew a man who earned a new "type rating" at an age when many others would be hanging up their flight jackets. His real name was Bob Rawlins, but he had earned the nickname "Dark Cloud" because he always seemed to have a doom and gloom attitude.

By vocation Bob was an insurance salesman, but he was an excellent golfer by avocation. When I knew him, Bob had won the National Seniors Amateur golf title. To be eligible to play in the Senior Division of the tournament, the participants have to be over fifty-five years old.

Nothing ever seemed to go right in Bob's life. If he shot a 72 when playing golf, all he could think about was the two shots that went badly and prevented him from scoring 70. He was never satisfied, even when he was national champion in the Senior Division.

After I spoke at the seminar where I met Bob, he told me that he had always wanted to go on the PGA Seniors Tour. He explained that since he had won the Senior Division Amateur title, he had actually been invited to play in a few matches on the PGA tour.

I said, "Gosh, Bob, why don't you just do it?"

"I can't go out and play against Arnold Palmer and Julius Boros," he said. "They're the greatest in the game. Besides, they didn't start when they were nearly sixty, as I am now."

I said, "What happens if you get to be sixty and you stop living for the day? Besides, how old do you feel?"

He thought for a moment and said, "Yeah, you know, you're right. I'm going to do it."

Bob started going to some of the tournaments to play for the wild card spots. They always had room for three or four players in each tournament, but he had to play numerous other aspirants to win one of those wild card spots. It was very expensive even to attempt this, and Bob had to absorb all the travel, hotel, and meal costs, and the high entry fees for the tournaments.

Many of the players Bob was competing against were sponsored by companies that pay players for wearing their clothes or insignia, or using their equipment. Bob was on his own, but he landed a wild card entry position in a couple of the tournaments.

The rules of the tour exempted the top fifty money winners from tryouts to play in the tournament. Bob knew that if he could get into the top fifty, he would be in a much better position because, instead of vying for a wild card spot, he would be able to enter any PGA tournament automatically.

At the end of each season, the PGA holds a wild card tournament for three or four exempt slots. These allow the winners to enter any PGA tournament even though they are not among the top fifty money winners. Bob thought this would be a great way for him to change his current situation, in which he was paying his own expenses and sometimes not earning an entry position.

Whenever people move forward to take on the challenge of doing something on a higher level than before, they usually improve to match the surrounding environment. Bob was no exception.

As good as he had been when he won the National Senior Amateur title, he continued to improve on the PGA tour. At the end of the season, when they held the tournament for the wild card exemption spots, Bob won one of the four positions. He was sixty-one at the time. He ended the tour as the number-fifty money winner, though he had played against such golfing legends as Jack Nicklaus, Arnold Palmer, and Lee Trevino. He even finished the season ahead of Arnold Palmer in tournament winnings!

Because of his success, Bob was able to get a sponsor for the following season. The sponsorship money, combined with his being number fifty and gaining automatic entry, ensured that his next season was even more successful.

Many people in Bob's position, when confronted with the hurdle of having to compete against Arnold Palmer, would have thought, "Why even try?" That's like spending your life thinking things always remain the same.

Instead, at age sixty, Bob put out enormous effort to grow and expand his universe, and succeeded in adding a new type rating. What matters is the next challenge, the next hurdle, the next tournament. If there was no chance for someone like Bob to gain exemption status in the face of competition from Arnold Palmer, they wouldn't even hold the tournament. Each challenge must be faced for what it is now, not what it might have been years ago. I was glad to see that my seminars had turned Bob "Dark Cloud" Rawlins into a self-encourager.

No matter what your age, keep moving forward. You can't change the past. All you can do is live in the present and use your current moments as well as possible. When you learn how to do that, you will be a successful self-encourager, but while you are learning, you can probably use the services of a certified flight instructor.

*Pilots can only take instruction from other pilots who have been certified by the FAA as instructors. Flight instructors are not necessarily the best pilots, nor are they the most experienced. The determining factor is successfully completing the training to teach others to fly.*

---

# 14
## CERTIFIED FLIGHT INSTRUCTOR

Certified flight instructors (CFIs) are the ones who create emergencies so that we can learn, pushing us to do things we wouldn't normally do. You can gain an important advantage in life by choosing the right people as instructors.

I have known many people from whom I expected to get a great boost and was disappointed, and I have picked up incredible encouragement when I least expected it. To get the most out of life, you've got to learn the difference, then take the best of what the good ones show you. You can also learn from the bad ones, even if all you learn is how *not* to treat other people.

How do you sort out the good ones from the bad ones? When they scream impatiently at you or put you in situations that push your limits too far, you're probably dealing with people who don't have your best interests at heart. Poor flight instructors are often on the job only as a stepping stone to move on to their next level, and they may well resent what they're doing in their lives when they are instructing you.

Choose your mentors wisely. Look for those who love the thrill

150

of teaching or who want to pass on their knowledge as a legacy. You will be able to sense which ones care enough to see you grow.

## HEROES DON'T ALWAYS MAKE GOOD TEACHERS

When I was a kid, one of my biggest heroes was Mickey Mantle. One day I was invited to be in a commercial for a new toy called "Mickey Mantle's Backyard Baseball." I was thrilled that the commercial was to be filmed at Mantle's house in Dallas.

The day we went to film the commercial it snowed. We couldn't film a baseball commercial in the snow, so the shoot was postponed. We were sitting in the car and we asked if we could go to the house to meet Mickey and get his autograph. I was crushed to hear that Mickey said we couldn't come in, but I figured we'd get his autograph when we came back.

The weather was perfect on the day we were to go back to shoot the commercial. We were very excited about being in a commercial and meeting Mickey Mantle. I was so anxious to get his autograph, I could hardly wait.

When all the boys who were going to be in the commercial were finally at the house, we learned that Mickey still wouldn't give out autographs. One of the boys finally pestered Mickey enough that he grudgingly signed one, but then he refused to do it for the rest of us. I have never forgotten my disappointment, but I learned that hero worship is not a good standard for choosing a mentor.

People who excel at something are not necessarily good at teaching it, nor do they always want to teach it, and sometimes they don't want to teach at the time you need to learn. I have seen the disappointment when people automatically assume their bosses will be good teachers. A good mentor must be actively sought; teaching is a two-way street that works best when both of you are ready.

When you are stuck with a CFI who doesn't serve your needs, you can offer feedback that you are not responding well to the instruction. If a mentor has been impatient, say that you respond best to positive encouragement and thoughtful, constructive help. Sometimes a direct approach will make clear what serves you best.

I believe that we choose most of the circumstances and people in our lives. Few of us are truly powerless. After all, you have already made a series of choices that led you where you are now and placed you among the people with whom you associate. If you are enduring an insufferable boss or an intolerable instructor, you have made choices somewhere along the way to place them in your life and you can make choices to replace them.

Even when you think you're stuck with those you detest, you can get away from them and spend time with boosters. If your life is filled with people who make you miserable, you may have chosen to continue being around them because of a benefit you receive from the relationship.

On the other hand, you cannot spend your life jumping from one instructor to another. When you can, it's best to try to iron out differences and work out compromises. Sometimes the only option is to move on to another instructor or another location.

Because life moves and changes you, there will be times when you will outgrow an instructor. This might happen when you have benefited from the relationship but the instructor is unable to take you all the way to your planned destination.

This is a common occurrence with talented athletes, especially those bound for the Olympics, and there are usually two reasons for it. First, a coach who was excellent for getting the athlete to an advanced stage in the early years may lack the skill to move the athlete to the level of Olympic performance. Second, the coach may have the knowledge to take someone to Olympic level, but may be unable to communicate effectively the high level of skill needed by a successful Olympian.

## LEARNING FROM YOUR OWN MISTAKES

There is no better learning aid than to make your own mistakes. A good CFI will let you go far astray before bailing you out, and then will help you analyze what would have happened if the CFI had not been there. When pushing your limits, you've got to trust your CFI and be ready to follow his instructions without question.

Good instructors will help you make controlled mistakes by giving you "contingency drills." In flying, they often do that by saying, in the middle of an otherwise uneventful flight, "You just lost your engine. What are you going to do now?" The first few times that happens, you have no idea what you'd do. You may look around frantically for an emergency field, and check the wind for landing direction, but it's too late. Flight instructors have a knack for pulling that trick when they know you are flying too low to land safely.

Each time an instructor pulls the engine-failure contingency, the memory stays with you. At first, you may be too busy learning the basics of handling the plane to do much that is rational. Eventually, after being embarrassed several times, you find yourself integrating an emergency landing plan with normal flying maneuvers. Finally, the day comes when you are confidently flying a near perfect maneuver at the CFI's direction and he yanks off the power and screams, "Okay, you just lost your engine. What are you going to do now?"

This time, you calmly respond, "I've had an eye on that field a couple of miles to the north, and with the wind blowing from the south, I'll glide up over it and turn back to land south after I clear the power lines near the fence."

Even if you are highly competent, you can use your own instructors as pilots use CFIs. In the airlines, even the most experienced pilots would get rusty without continual instruction. The top golfers on the PGA tour also take lessons regularly, as do nearly all professionals, especially athletes and performing artists. Nevertheless, many of us are reluctant to take instruction in the very things that make our livelihood possible.

## ARE YOU THE "WGA" OR THE SUBSONIC CONCORDE?

While my experience meeting Mickey Mantle soured me on holding up heroes as role models, I later met another superstar who was a master of positive thinking.

Paul Shoop is a good friend of mine, with whom I grew up during my high school years. We got to know each other on the school football team. His father was Captain Glen Shoop, one of the lead pilots for Braniff Airlines.

Because of my aspirations to become an airline pilot, Paul's dad became a sort of hero to me. Sometimes when I visited Paul, I'd put on his dad's hat and coat and imagine myself being a jet airline pilot. Over the years, I spent hours hanging around the Shoop house talking about flying with my hero.

At one point in the 1970s, Braniff Airlines cut a deal with British Airways to initiate through-plane service from London to Dallas on the Concorde. The SST would be flown by British pilots from London to New York or to Washington, D.C., where Braniff pilots would take over and fly the plane to Dallas and back to either New York or Washington. On the East Coast, the Braniff crew returned the plane to the British crew, who flew it to London.

### Stuck in First Gear

Because of noise restrictions, the Braniff pilots were not able to fly the Concorde at supersonic speed over U.S. territory. Nonetheless, it was a thrill for a Texan to be at the controls of the world's fastest airliner.

Since Captain Shoop was one of Braniff's most senior pilots, he was among the first to get to fly the Concorde between Dallas and its other two domestic destinations. I thought this had to be a unique experience for any pilot, and I asked Captain Shoop what it was like to fly the Concorde. His answer surprised me.

"It's like driving a Ferrari Formula One racer in first gear only. You have so much power at your fingertips and you sit there, cruising along at the same speed as any other airliner, just staring at those throttles and thinking, 'Boy, I sure would like to jam those babies to the firewall and feel the afterburners kick in!' "

Can you imagine how frustrating it would be to have the controls of the world's most powerful jetliner at your fingertips, and be denied the opportunity to use it as it was designed? Have you ever experienced anything like that yourself? Yes, you probably have.

Many people go through life and never touch the power they have at their fingertips, remaining content with partial performance, though they've got afterburners built in. A properly chosen mentor in your life can show you how to kick in your personal afterburners.

*Meeting the "WGA"*

After high school, Paul Shoop went to college and then to law school. After he became a lawyer, he moved to California and settled in Malibu, where his longtime love for athletics led him to a firm that represented many noted sports figures. Paul excelled at what he did and soon attracted some of the best-known names in sports as his clients.

One day when I was visiting Paul, we were at a restaurant having lunch and in walked Bruce Jenner, the 1976 Olympic gold medal decathlon winner. I was awed because I always thought that winning a gold medal in the decathlon took a Superman who would be the best overall athlete in the world. It turned out that Paul knew Bruce and invited him to join us for lunch. I was pleased to discover that Bruce was a delightful person, and we had a pleasant lunch.

After Bruce left, Paul told me that all his close friends in Malibu called him "WGA," which stands for "World's Greatest Athlete." That made perfect sense to me, but it turned out that "WGA" was a private joke between Bruce and his friends because Bruce is not really a great athlete. For instance, when a group of people get together on the beach to play volleyball, Bruce isn't the first player chosen for a team. He's not the best player in their group, and he does not stand out from the crowd when they play other sports together. If you didn't know who he was, Paul said, you'd never guess his extraordinary athletic accomplishment.

Outside of winning a gold medal in the decathlon, Bruce Jenner is much like you and me. He's an average guy who gathered all of his abilities and marshaled them for the performance of a lifetime.

What is happening in your life? Are you an average person like Bruce Jenner who is reaching down inside of yourself and pulling out a spectacular performance? Or are you flying through life like the Braniff pilots had to fly the Concorde, throttled back and flying at far less than what your peak performance could be? If you are not flying at full throttle, have the self-confidence and foresight to tap the resources of a coach, instructor, or mentor in your life.

## THE POWER OF POSITIVE THINKING

During the mid-1980s, there was a wave of "positive thinking rallies," which toured the country selling tickets for programs featuring speakers such as Dr. Norman Vincent Peale, Art Linkletter, or Zig Zigler. The rallies were advertised months in advance and the tickets were reasonably priced because the rallies were held in big arenas that held tens of thousands of people.

I was the emcee at some of these events, hired to introduce the featured speaker. It was a wonderful experience for me to work with so many of the day's best-known inspirational speakers, and to make presentations before such large audiences.

There was no script because every rally was different, and my job required me to be in control of the audience. I had to take account of what the last speaker had said and what the next speaker would say. I gauged the audience's moods and reactions so that I knew if they needed an anecdote to warm things up, or a joke to break the ice, or to move quickly on to the next speaker.

The first time I got to do a rally with Dr. Norman Vincent Peale was in Baton Rouge, Louisiana. Before the rally began, I met with him and asked how he liked to be introduced. He said he liked "a really fired-up introduction." That wasn't hard to do because Dr. Peale was the dean of positive speakers, and the audience would have been fired up merely by the thought that he was next. By the time I was ready to introduce Dr. Peale, I had every member of that audience on the edges of their seats.

My last words before he came out were "Ladies and gentlemen, please welcome Dr. Norman Vincent Peale." Instantly, the entire crowd jumped to their feet and broke into a wild standing ovation. I walked across the stage to where he would make his entrance. When he appeared, the crowd went even wilder. I had planned to shake his hand, then exit the stage. Instead, Dr. Peale took hold of my arm and pulled me over to the speaker's lectern with him.

The roaring applause continued for a while, then finally settled down, and the people took their seats. There I was, standing next to the lectern with him, and he simply started his talk. I thought to myself, "I shouldn't be standing out here! These people don't want to see or hear me." But Dr. Peale just continued for a minute or two with his usual speech.

It seemed like an hour to me. He went on as if I weren't there, except that he didn't let go of my arm. I felt awkward and completely ill at ease.

Finally, he interrupted his speech and said, "You know, ladies and gentlemen, I've been introduced thousands of times over the years, by countless emcees. I want you to know that in all those years, I have never been introduced more enthusiastically or positively by anyone than I have today." And, with that, the entire audience stood up and gave *me* a standing ovation!

Moments before, I was practically cursing him under my breath for putting me in such an awkward spot. Seconds later, I discovered that he wanted to share his thanks with the whole arena, and in doing so, he gave me one of the highlights and one of the most memorable moments of my life.

Sometimes we are too quick to judge things. Maybe we're feeling uncomfortable and wondering why we're in a particular situation. Avoiding a negative conclusion for a few minutes may lead us to a triumphant moment in our lives.

The most valuable assistance I received from Dr. Peale came at another rally later on the same tour, in Corpus Christi, Texas. I had a speaking engagement in Austin, Texas, the night before the rally.

*157*

My son, Kelly, who was ten years old at the time, was with me on that trip. After my speech in Austin, we had to drive for about three hours to reach Corpus Christi. Kelly and I left at about ten o'clock at night and he fell asleep right away.

I expected to get into Corpus Christi at about one in the morning. Instead, when I got to San Antonio, the weather turned to thick fog. I could barely see and had to slow down to ten or fifteen miles per hour to stay on the road. I drove on, hoping I would soon leave the fog behind, but it continued all the way to Corpus Christi. I didn't get there until seven o'clock in the morning, and I was due to speak at eight.

As I was creeping along through the fog, I knew I would barely make it to the speech and that I would be exhausted from the all-night drive. Staring out the windshield at that gray nothingness that enveloped every inch of my path, I was upset about the delay and inconvenience. Then I remembered a story that Dr. Peale told about when he was a young boy.

He was in New York, on the Staten Island Ferry with his mother, and they were in the midst of a thick fog. His mother told him to see how beautiful the lights were in the fog, and to listen to the foghorns of the passing ships out in the harbor. He always remembered that trip because he was amazed that his mother could see beauty in every place she was and in everything she did.

As I was crawling across the shrouded Texas countryside, all I could see was the ugly fog that impeded my travel, and I wished it would go away. I was too upset and tired to see any beauty. I only wanted to hurry up and get there. Remembering Dr. Peale's story helped a little, but I simply couldn't get past being upset.

When I got to Corpus Christi, I went straight to where I was going to speak. I walked in and was greeted immediately by Dr. Peale. When he saw me, he said, "Patrick O'Dooley, are you ready to go this morning?"

I said, "Dr. Peale, I don't feel well. I'm late because of the fog and I'm exhausted. I was thinking about the story of you and your mother in the fog on the Staten Island Ferry, but I still didn't see any good in the fog I had to drive through last night."

"God made the fog," Dr. Peale said. "The fog is good. Let's go do it!"

Now there's a certified flight instructor for life. If you can get help from upbeat people like Dr. Peale, the fog you encounter won't matter. With a positive attitude, you will be able to fly full-throttle through every day of your life as if it were CAVU — "ceiling and visibility unlimited."

*The ultimate enjoyment in flying is viewing the world from a lofty perch when the weather is perfect. All pilots dream of hearing the weather briefer use the spoken acronym for CAVU weather, "It's cavoo all the way."*

# 15
# CEILING AND VISIBILITY UNLIMITED

The weather changes daily in flying, but in life we often can make our own weather. We do that by choosing to view life as if it carried a daily weather forecast of CAVU, ceiling and visibility unlimited. While there's plenty of doom and gloom out there, no one else can tell you how to feel. In other words, take the blinders off so you can get the most out of each day and see all the good in your life.

## W. MITCHELL — CAVU THROUGH THE FOG

A man I admire greatly is named W. Mitchell. He was a young, strong, and healthy man living in San Francisco until one day he fell while riding his motorcycle and slid under a truck. The accident caused a fire in which he was burned so extensively over most of his body that his ears and fingers were burned off.

Despite his terrible injuries, W. Mitchell maintained a strong and positive attitude throughout his long and painful recovery. Then, instead of wallowing in sorrow and self-pity, he moved to

Colorado and started a new business from which he became a millionaire. He parlayed his business success into the political arena and became the mayor of Crested Butte, Colorado.

Despite the grotesque injuries to his exterior, W. Mitchell lived a rich life internally. He realized that his mind and soul had not been burned, only his body. On the inside, he was still the same person as he was before his accident.

His injuries improved enough for W. Mitchell to learn to fly, and he bought his own airplane. He flew all over the country, giving motivational speeches that encouraged people to work through whatever troubles they encountered.

Then, while flying himself between speeches in his airplane, his plane crashed and he suffered a serious back injury that left him paralyzed from the waist down. Even if the burns from the motorcycle accident hadn't killed his spirit, you might expect that his paralysis would put him permanently into a state of depression.

However, his powerfully positive attitude remained even after the second accident. W. Mitchell still travels the country as a motivational speaker, helping people to become self-encouragers. His speeches are now more effective than ever because he can say to his audiences, "If I can do it, you can do it!" How many people can argue with that?

If you could run a computer program that rated us on our physical and mental abilities, and weighed them against our attitude, I bet that W. Mitchell would be number one. I've never heard of anyone else who is such a strong self-encourager and has done so much with such formidable challenges.

W. Mitchell's favorite saying is "I never focus on the thousand things I can't do. I focus on the nine thousand things I *can* do." His message is that we are tougher than we think we are, and we can do far more than we've ever imagined. However, most of us never have our limits tested, and we cruise along using only a fraction of what is available inside us, like the Braniff pilots who flew the Concorde at partial throttle.

## CRISIS AS SEEN BY THE CHINESE

You probably know that the Chinese language is made up of thousands of complex characters. Many of the characters are obtained by adding one or more other characters together. The Chinese symbol for *crisis* is formed by the combination of two characters meaning *danger* and *opportunity*.

When you encounter a situation in your life that you see as a crisis, remember two things. First, remember that the Chinese don't even have a word for crisis. Instead, they see every dangerous situation as bringing an opportunity with it. Second, remember the opportunities that came into W. Mitchell's life as a result of the dangers he encountered.

## YOU'RE A FIVE

I have a numbers game I like to ask people to play with me at my seminars. I ask them, "On a scale of one to five, with five being the B.E.S.T. and one being a complete nerd, where would you rate yourself?" I want to know how they see themselves in life in general. It's a quick way to get an answer to the question, "Are you merely getting by, or are you actually on your way to someplace special?"

Sometimes people will rate themselves as a one or a two, but most people rate themselves as a four or a five. When I find people who have rated themselves at less than five, I tell them that they truly are fives, and that I can prove it.

Take any number between one and ten . . . any number, it doesn't matter. Now take that number and double it. Take that result and add ten to it. Next, divide that result by two. Now subtract the number you originally had in mind.

I was right. You are a five, aren't you?

I like this exercise because it illustrates that life is nothing but a game. You may not realize that you're a five, but you are, and you'll see that you are if you refuse to be intimidated by life and if you become a self-encourager. If you ever begin to doubt yourself, remember, I can prove that you are always a five.

Self-encouragers don't hole up and hide from the things in their lives that go wrong. Instead, they always focus on the thousands of things that are right. They see the things in life that are good and get the most out of their strengths. We have enough in us all the time to be fives. We just have to reach down into ourselves so we can see it and believe it.

I've developed a list of tips to help keep you motivated even when the weather in your life is turbulent. Over the years, I have come to see this list as gems that best help me to be a self-encourager. I call them my *Eight and One-Half Ways to Stay Motivated.*

## EIGHT AND ONE-HALF WAYS TO STAY MOTIVATED

*1. Watch what you read.*

As you fill your mind with thoughts, they manifest themselves into actions. If you fill your mind with doom and gloom, then that is likely to be what you will experience. It's not possible to plant bad seeds and get good crops. Similarly, the ancient proverb tells us, "As ye thinketh, so shall ye be."

I encourage you to read something inspirational every day and plant your mind with all the good seeds you can. Do this first thing in the morning to start your day right and get you going on a positive note. Then, do it a second time at the end of the day before you go to bed, so you will have something positive to think about as you drift off to sleep.

*2. Listen to uplifting cassettes.*

You may love to listen to music when you drive, but if you use some of your driving time to fill your mind with the words of positive, uplifting, motivational speakers, you will feel even better than you do from listening to your favorite music. Your local library probably has a great collection of cassette audio tape programs on file. If not, the information desk librarian will help you find sources that will rent the tapes to you.

*3. Associate with positive, uplifting people.*

You're known by the company you keep. If you hang around with ne'er-do-wells, you will begin seeing things from their perspective and you may begin to think that life is rotten. If, on the other hand, you hang around with winners and upbeat people, you will see things from their perspective and begin to think that life is a joyous and wondrous event.

*4. Exercise regularly.*

Countless studies have demonstrated that people who exercise at least thirty minutes at a time, at least three times a week, think more clearly, feel better, and are more upbeat about life. They generally live longer than people who don't exercise, while enjoying a happier and more productive life.

*5. Walk 19 percent faster.*

By walking faster than a group, you become a pacesetter and you automatically appear to be a leader. When you see someone walking fast, don't you wonder, "Where's that person going? I wonder what that person is doing." Be a pacesetter. Why should you walk 19 percent faster? See rule number 8½.

*6. Sing in the shower.*

This idea came to me from Dr. William James, who says, "You don't sing because you're happy, you're happy because you sing." The great thing about singing in the shower is that you do it the first thing in the morning and it puts you in a good mood to start the day. You don't have to be a good singer, either, and you don't have to be by yourself. You'll be amazed how singing in the shower will affect you and those around you.

*7. Sit in the front row and volunteer.*

When you attend a meeting or a seminar, you will get more out of it and be more attuned to what goes on if you sit in the front row. If you volunteer answers to the speaker, you become the one that the speaker looks at and because you are actively involved, you will get more out of it.

164

*8. Do something nice for somebody else.*

This is particularly good when you do something to help someone who cannot do anything for you. Find something you can give, unconditionally, knowing you are doing it only for the act and not out of any ulterior motive.

This idea is what led me to start my "Tip of the Month Club," where I give a brand-new twenty-dollar bill each month to someone who does an especially nice job for me. When you give to others, *you* become the winner. You cannot give for long without it coming back to you many times over.

*8½. Be different.*

That's why I called this one eight and one-half instead of nine. Simply being different can help you stay motivated. You might ask, "How can I be different?" It can be in the little things you do. For example, I always back into parking spaces because everyone else pulls in facing forward.

At one point in my life, I was selling photocopying machines for IBM. This is a highly competitive market, and I knew that all the people I saw were visited by Xerox and Kodak salespeople as well. I decided that I was going to be different, so they would remember me. What I came up with was to introduce myself as "Patrick O'Dooley, Reproduction Specialist." Many times I got a lot of funny looks, but one thing was always certain: they never forgot who I was.

Recently, I had to arrange a meeting with the head of the Dallas Convention and Tourism Bureau. She called and said, "When can you get over here to see me?"

"I can be there tomorrow at 10:17," I answered.

There was a long pause. I knew what she was thinking, but she didn't say anything except, "Okay, 10:17 tomorrow will be fine."

Clearly, when you make an appointment to be somewhere important at 10:17, you'd better be there at 10:17. The next day, when I arrived, she was standing in the doorway, looking at her watch. "Thank goodness! Boy, am I glad you are on time. I've been a nervous wreck all morning waiting to find out if you were really going to be here at 10:17." As we walked back to her office, we passed a lot of those little cubicle offices and all along the way, people kept asking her, "Is that the 10:17 guy?"

I stood out in her mind simply by approaching a little differently something that could have been like all the other appointments she makes. She met me at the door, and everyone in the office knew I was coming.

## IT'S THE LITTLE THINGS

In your flight through life, the little things you do for yourself will make you a self-encourager and the little things you do for others can encourage them tremendously. That's why none of the tips on my list of ways to stay motivated are major steps; they're all small actions that you can take every day.

I recently witnessed an outstanding example of someone adding a little thing to life that had a great impact on a lot of people, yet took only seconds. I was on an American Airlines plane to Los Angeles, and after we landed, the lead flight attendant, who had attended one of my seminars, ran through her usual announcements and thanked everyone for flying her airline. Then she added, "As you're leaving, here's a little thought for the day: 'Success is a journey, not a destination.' Here's to your wonderful journey." As the passengers deplaned, at least twenty of them stopped to thank her for adding that little extra to their day.

Our world is filled with people who believe they haven't the time to encourage others. However, elevating the stature of others can increase your own stature even more than tooting your own horn.

William Gladstone served as the British prime minister from 1868 to 1874. His successor was Benjamin Disraeli, who served from 1874 to 1880. Politically and personally, these two men were at opposite poles. Gladstone was a pompous, self-indulgent Conservative, and Disraeli was a wily, gentlemanly Tory.

A young woman had the unique opportunity of dining with each of them on successive nights. When asked for her impression of the two men, she replied, "When I left the dining room after sitting next to Mr. Gladstone, I thought he was the cleverest man in England. But after sitting next to Mr. Disraeli, I thought *I* was the cleverest woman in England."

You can help yourself and everyone you meet by looking for all the good you already have in yourself and all the good in others. To become a self-encourager, decide to be responsible for your own happiness and to share your joy with everyone you know. Every day you have the choice of whether to let the turbulence in your life make you unhappy or to fly through it.

To be happy, you need to make a commitment to be your B.E.S.T. every day. My definition of B.E.S.T. is to "Begin Everyday Selecting Tremendous." From the first moment you are awake, begin the day by making a choice to "select tremendous" for yourself because there is an orderly sequence of events in the shaping of our lives. Here is how it works:

As I think, I make choices.
As I make choices, I form habits.
As I form habits, I fix the direction of my life.
So, if I am to live differently, I must form new habits.
If I am to form new habits, I must make new choices.
If I am to make new choices, I must do new thinking.
It is more important to *do* your BEST than to *be* the BEST.


## *THE MAN IN THE MIRROR*

I picked up my best tip for the self-encourager when I was in Carmel, California, for a speaking engagement. My wife, Beverly, and I were walking downtown on the main street, looking at all the wonderful shops. Suddenly, we looked up and saw the mayor of Carmel. Do you know who the mayor of Carmel was?

Clint Eastwood.

However, that's not how I saw him. The person I saw walking toward me on that sidewalk was Dirty Harry, the character Eastwood made famous in his long string of successful movies. All I could think of was that he would walk up to us, stick his hand in his jacket and pull out that cannon that he calls a gun, point it at us, and say, "Go ahead, make my day!"

That classic line made famous by Eastwood is known all around the world. The day we saw him on the street, I started thinking of Eastwood's trademark line in a different context. As a self-encourager, get up in the morning, look in the mirror, and say, "Go ahead, make my day!"

Don't let the weather make your day. Don't let the traffic on the way to work or the people you work with make your day. Instead, get up and Begin Everyday Selecting Tremendous for yourself.

If you have trouble deciding who's responsible for your happiness, here's a poem that will help you when you stare at your face each morning:

### The Man in the Glass

When you get what you want in your struggle for self
    And the world makes you king for a day,
Just go to the mirror and look at yourself
    And see what that man has to say.

For it isn't your father or mother or wife
    Whose judgment upon you must pass.
The fellow whose verdict counts most in your life
    Is the one staring back from the glass.

You may be like Jack Horner and chisel a plum
    And think you're a wonderful guy.
But the man in the glass says you're only a bum
    If you can't look him straight in the eye.

He's the fellow to please — never mind all the rest,
    For he's with you clear to the end.
And you've passed your most dangerous, difficult test
    If the man in the glass is your friend.

You may fool the whole world down the pathway of years
    And get pats on the back as you pass.

But your final reward will be heartache and tears
If you've cheated the man in the glass.

When you become a self-encourager, you won't ever again be cheated by the man in the glass. Instead, you'll *Begin Everyday Selecting Tremendous* for yourself by saying loud and clear into that mirror, "GO AHEAD, MAKE MY DAY!"

# About the Author

Patrick O'Dooley is a native of Dallas, Texas. He attended the University of Oklahoma on an athletic scholarship, graduating with a degree in marketing. After serving in the U.S. Army overseas as an aviation officer, O'Dooley returned to Dallas, where he enjoyed a successful career in sales and sales management with IBM and Steelcase Furniture Corporation.

He is a charter member and past president of the North Texas Speakers Association. In addition, Patrick O'Dooley is a Certified Speaking Professional, the highest designation given by the National Speakers Association, on whose board of directors he has served. Today, the author is president of his own consulting and speaking firm.